From the **Girl** to the Redefined
WOMAN

From the **Girl** to the Redefined
WOMAN

Developing the Strength
to Go from a Breakdown
to a Breakthrough

TAYLOR B. COHEN

Cover photos by Motelewa Smith
Cover design by 360 Media Group
Page design by Win-Win Words

ISBN: 978-0-692-12072-9

Printed in the United States of America.

Contents

Acknowledgments

FIRST AND FOREMOST, I GIVE ALL PRAISE, THANKS, GLORY, AND honor to God, who truly is the head over my life. Without him, I am nothing. This book would not have been manifested had it not been for his placing the gift inside of me, giving me the vision, and then bestowing on me the power to execute.

To my amazing parents Elliott and Josette Cohen; I love you both from the bottom of my heart. Thank you for consistently pushing me into my purpose. Thank you for being the greatest parents in the world. I cannot imagine getting this far without you both there to provide guidance and support. Most importantly, thank you for covering me. Dad, thank you for teaching me the importance of developing and maintaining a relationship with Jesus Christ at such a young age. Thank you for showing me what it's like to be loved so that I didn't have to grow up seeking others to fill a void. Thank you for reminding me every day how much you loved me and how beautiful I am. Mom, thank you for showing me what it's like to be a wife, mother, and role model all in one. Your strength and faith in God are impeccable! I admire you, and I pray that I will continue to grow to be as strong as you are. Thank you for loving me, praying for me, and always being there for me! You are the best mommy ever!

To my brother Donavon and my baby sister Mya. I love you both from the bottom of my heart! You both have been my inspiration in so many ways and during so many seasons of my life. Don, man, nobody will ever understand our relationship. It's like the older we get, the closer we get. You are so anointed in what God has called you to do. Your authentic fire for God just sparks my spirit. Thank you for being the greatest big brother, role model, protector, friend, and prayer partner that you are. I look up to you in so many ways. You are a *great* husband to my sister-in-law Candice and a great role model to so many young people in this generation. I'm proud of you and I love you!

Mya—my little mini-me. My little songbird. I'm so proud of you. Your voice is so unique! Your confidence and hard work inspire me. You are going to be an amazing make-up artist one day; I can just see it now. Big Sis loves you with all her heart, and I will always be there for you. Thank you for all the times you've called me to pray for you and give you advice. I strive to be the best woman that I can be because I know you watch everything that I do. I love you!

To the rest of my immediate family (grandparents, aunts, uncles, cousins), I love each one of you. I have a special relationship with each of you individually. I love my crazy, sangin', and joke-crackin' family! You all have pushed me, encouraged me, blessed me in so many ways. I wouldn't trade this family for *anything*!

To my second family, the Walker Family (Bishop Joseph W. Walker III, Dr. Stephaine M. Walker, Jovanni W. Walker, Joseph W. Walker IV), I love you! From the moment that I connected with you back in May 2016, I knew that it was God. I was scared, nervous, mind-blown, excited, and grateful all in one. Each of you have changed my life *forever*! Thank you for allowing God to speak to you on giving me a chance. Dr. Steph—thank you for being an amazing mentor to young women like myself. Thank you for trusting me to serve your family in the capacity that I did; thank you for trusting me in your home; and, most importantly, thank you for allowing me to serve alongside *you*. You have inspired me, given me wisdom, encouraged me, corrected me, loved me, and been there for me when I needed you the most. You have shown me what it's like to make things happen! You are an amazing and beautiful woman, wife, mother, mentor, and friend. I admire you, and I love you! Bishop, thank you for your leadership. Since coming to Mount Zion, I have received so much word and revelation, and that has helped to transform me into the woman that I am today. Thank you for giving me an opportunity to have a seat at the table among some amazing and influential people. Thank you for the many times you've listened to me and prayed for me. Thank you for showing me what greatness looks like! Thank you for always giving me sound wisdom. I appreciate you for being so kind to me. You are an amazing husband, father, pastor, and inspiration to so many people around the world. I love you! JoJo, I will always love you, my little princess. You will always be my baby! You were always glued to my hip and that's what I loved the most. You always knew how to make me laugh and brighten up my spirit if I was having a bad day. You are so precious, beautiful, and intelligent! I love you! Baby Walker, I was so happy when I found out your mommy and daddy were having you! You are going to be something so special. Although you don't have a clue who I am, I love you!

To my best friends, Janelle, Morgan, and Dejah. You girls already know how we rock!!! Since the moment I shared with you my vision and that I was in the process of writing my first book, you were excited for me and gave me encouragement throughout the process. I love you three very much and thank you for always being there for me. Thank you for showing me the true definition of friendship, but, most importantly, thank you for loving me and accepting me for who I am!!!! Love you, sissies!!!!

To the rest of my support team, I love you all! Thank you for your support, your prayers, your love, and your encouragement. You guys rock!!!!

Signed,
TayBrianne

A Letter to the Future Woman . . .

Hey, Beautiful,

I can just imagine what you're going to be like. Your future is so bright; don't you let anyone tell you any different. You are essential, you are unique, and you are one of a kind. I know you're probably thinking why it took so long for you to arrive, right? But remember, there will come a day when you will realize that all the circumstances—the hurt, the lonely nights, the struggles, the challenges, the uncertainties, and the bad days—that your younger self is experiencing will be worthwhile. Remember, it's only temporary.

One day, the future you will look back at all that has transpired and will be glad that the younger you was chosen for it. To the future woman, I speak that you will let your light shine! To the younger you, continue to push your way out of darkness and into that light, no matter how bad it hurts! To the both of you, above all else, continue to love yourself and remain true to you! Smile and be thankful for everything good and bad. No one ever said that the road would be easy; if it were, nobody would appreciate the value of life. You are simply amazing, and there is a special gift that God has placed deep down inside of you that separates you from other people. Soon enough, God will reveal it to you through your future you! I guarantee you, it's coming! Remain that beautiful Queen you are. There's a lot for you to see on this journey, and, trust me, you haven't even seen everything yet. Embrace it and enjoy every moment of it!

Until next time,
TayBrianne XOXO

Introduction: The Broken Girl

"I would like to be known as an intelligent woman,
a courageous woman, a loving woman,
a woman who teaches by being."

— MAYA ANGELOU

I T WAS A VERY COLD FRIDAY NIGHT, ROUGHLY AROUND 3:00 A.M., and my heart was pounding. I knew that being drunk and seeing him that night was not such a good idea. Something in me screamed, *"No, Tay, you better not!"* But the other part of me was eager to see him again. That whisper in my ear and his hand touching my thigh as I walked out of the club brought back so many memories; I just couldn't seem to resist the temptation. I was too weak, I was still vulnerable, everything was still fresh, and I hadn't fully recovered from all that had happened a few months earlier, so I gave in. My flesh won, and, to be honest with you, I didn't try to fight back, either! I hopped out of bed as soon as my phone began buzzing. He texted me to let me know he was headed back to his apartment. Without hesitation, I immediately sent him a reply, "I'm on my way . . ."

Why did I have to see him that night at the club? Without the text, maybe he wouldn't have crossed my mind. As I began scrambling through my closet, I chose to grab the jacket with the hood on it. I was already ashamed that I was creeping out at the wee hours in the morning. I wanted to make sure no one would notice me, so I had to figure out a way to disguise myself.

Instead of going out the front, as usual, and walking all the way around, I took the back way, because it was a straight shot from my apartment to his. Each step I took, I could feel the beat of my heart getting faster and faster. I thought, *What am I doing?* as I continued to get closer to his apartment building. How did I even end up in communication with a person I said I was never going to speak to again?

As I approached his apartment door, I could feel my palms beginning to sweat. I kept looking back at my apartment, thinking I should just turn around and go home, but I kept moving toward his door. By the time that I reached it, my heart was racing, my head was spinning, and I felt myself getting ready to go into panic mode. I took a few deep breaths to try to calm down (inhale and exhale), but it didn't seem to help. What was I scared of? Scared because I just knew I was making the biggest mistake of my entire life. Scared because one whisper, one "I miss you," one "Let me see you," led me back down a dark path on which I didn't belong. Scared because God gave me every reason to leave this guy alone, but I didn't want to be obedient. I wanted to do things my own way. I wanted to fill that empty space with what I "thought" felt good.

I stood there for a moment just staring at the apartment number on the side of the door—3308. That was the apartment number that I had memorized after having been there so many times. The apartment where three of his roommates all knew me very well. They would see me on campus and would yell across campus, "*You coming over tonight?!*" The same apartment number where not just one but multiple women would be in and out of. That same apartment that I creeped to only when it was late at night. The apartment where I fell into a trap that stripped away my identity.

My hands began shaking as I pulled out my phone to dial his number. It rang once, and then it rang a second time. I was hoping that it would keep ringing so that I could just turn around and make my way back home. After the third ring, he picked up, and I cleared my throat. "Open up the door, I'm outside." I stood there with my legs shaking and my heart beating fast as I heard his footsteps getting closer. The minute that he opened the door, disbelief struck me that we were, again, actually standing face to face. This was after all those times I had told him I hated him, that I didn't want to have anything to do with him anymore and how I would never speak to him, let alone see him again. Yet, there I stood, right in front of him.

After months of not seeing this guy, I stepped into the room that had once brought me to the lowest, darkest place of my life. It was that place where I was a lost, young girl struggling to find the nearest exit because the door seemed to be so far away . . .

The Nearest Exit is *Closer* than You Think

Even when the exit door might seem far away, it's closer than you think. Better yet, it's right there in front of you. Ask yourself, *Am I courageous enough to walk through it?* Like some of you, I was that broken girl at one point in my life. Yes, it's true! I grew up as a preacher's kid and experienced sex before marriage. A couple of times! Yes, I struggled with my identity because of low self-esteem, peer pressure, negative influences, and lack of self-confidence. Yes, I have been in some of the worst places at the wrong time . . . that was me, too! Yes, I have been in the presence of alcohol and drugs. That was me! That was me because I allowed it to be me. At one point, I wanted it to be me. There was a lack of self-discipline.

There were many times when I had the opportunity to say "No" and walk away, but I allowed my peers to pressure me into saying, "OK, just one time . . . " I became so consumed in my environment that it began controlling my decisions, my behavior, my actions, and my emotions. Only when it brought me to what felt like the lowest point of my *life* did I know I wanted out! It was time to declare freedom over my own life.

I was searching for the nearest exit. It wasn't that it was so far away (it was right there in front of me); I just didn't have the strength to get up and walk to there! I was so concerned about the opinions of others, instead of focusing on what I needed for *me*! I was afraid of what I might lose along the way, but the moment where I stopped dwelling on the opinions of others and the dirt and damage that was done to me, I grabbed the key and unlocked the door!

Have you ever wondered what it would actually feel like if you unlocked the door to your freedom, peace, transformation, wholeness, and happiness? What it would feel like to be free from the pain, the lies, and the frustration from your past? Why are you so afraid of adjusting to something new; something that you've never had before? Why do you feel the need to back down now? Don't you think you've come too far to fall back into the cycles of internal destruction? Oh, I get it— you're scared of what it might cost you, right? You're content with living life as usual and thinking, *Oh, I'll get through this; I'm used to it.* Used to what? Crying late at night because you can't understand, why you? Used to settling for less than what you truly deserve? Used to giving up and quitting when times get difficult? Used to letting people talk you out of doing what you know is right for you?

At some point, you should say enough is enough! God is giving you access to freedom, but you must first be willing to grab the key. That is, take the first step. I wonder if you have looked at your current situation and thought, *I want better!* When was the last time you looked at yourself in the mirror and verbalized, *I'm not going to be that old girl anymore*, then believed it and took the necessary steps to depart from her?

Do you believe that a better life, better relationships, spiritual wholeness, a peace of mind, a transformed life, newness, and the redefined you are closer than you think? When God shows you a way out the first time, pay attention and obey! He showed me multiple times where the nearest exit was, while also telling me it was time to *evacuate* before things got worse. However, because I tried to run the show of my own life without instruction, I kept missing all the exit signs. It took me being knocked down to a lower-than-low point in my life before I realized it was time to stop playing games. It was time for the new!

A New Beginning

The new begins when you finally release the old. The Bible in 2 Corinthians 5:17 says, *"Therefore if any man be in Christ, he is a new creation, the old things have passed away and behold all things become new."* Your past and your struggles will always be parts of your story because without them, there would be no testimony to share. It does not mean that you must continue to live your life full of regrets and complaints about what you should have done or could have done or wished you would have done differently.

I spent different seasons of my life on different routes for different reasons to teach myself different lessons that would lead me to my destination. I learned valuable lessons that I will show you and teach you throughout the course of this book. It was a struggle for me, extremely tough. I cried, I prayed, I failed some tests, and I said things that probably never should have come out of my mouth. I was alone for a while, and some routes were extremely dark. I had to feel my way out of it, but the most important lesson from it all was that it was *necessary.* I don't know if I would have wanted it any other way than the way it was given to me; it was all connected to that moment where "new" would finally begin. I finally discovered who I really was, and, let me tell you, it took a long time!

Although I am still growing and learning so much about the woman that I am today, I have more wisdom now than I ever had. This book was written for anyone who has dealt with some of the same issues: peer pressure, negative influences, low self-esteem, manipulation, strongholds, lust, lack of confidence, brokenness, loneliness, bitterness, anger, unforgiveness, stress, and anxiety . . . and can't seem to find the courage within to come out. There is a way out. *Today* begins that day where you will break free from the chains that have tried to keep you locked away from your purpose and imprisoned from pursuing the Woman inside of you.

Let this book inspire you to get up and get out of your past and start climbing your way to your promise. This is for all the young queens who deserve a second chance, a fresh start, another opportunity to depart from the girl and arrive at their destination as the Redefined Woman. You're not quite sure how to get there. No worries . . . we will walk through this journey together! I am not a perfect person; I've made my fair share of mistakes. At one point, my life was all jacked up, but I am a firm believer in helping women rise together! Sometimes, all a woman needs is that extra support!

Think of this as your "start-over season." One profound thing I once heard is that God is the God of another Chance. We hear people say all the time that he is the God of a Second Chance. But what happens when we mess up the second time? Well, he's right there offering us another chance, and then when we screw up again he gives us *another* chance. That's called *grace!*

The route to your Redefining Moment will not be easy, and it will definitely be different than others, but remember that growth and change are always necessary. So, I invite you to join me as we journey through this together. Let me share with you how to go from your breakdown to your breakthrough. This might be a long trip, so get ready. In Revelation 12:11 it says, *"We overcome by the blood of the lamb and the word of our testimony,"* so don't be afraid to be honest with yourself and, once you get to your destination, to share with others how you made it!

It is my heart's desire that this will not be just another read, but a tool that guides you, stretches you, challenges you, and pushes you further to that Redefined Woman! Your freedom is knocking at your door, and Transformation is around the corner. You might have to scream, you might have to cry, and you might find out that you must leave some stuff behind. You might laugh, you might even have to shout, but whatever you need to do . . . *do it!* Don't bring anything with you on this trip. It might be a bumpy ride, and we might experience some dark roads along the way. I hope I didn't scare you; I just want to prepare you. OK, it's time! Are you ready?

From the **Girl** to the Redefined
WOMAN

1

The Process
of Becoming

*"If you belonged to the world, it would love you as its own.
As it is, you do not belong to the world, but I have chosen
you out of the world. This is why the world hates you."*

— John 15:19 New International Version (NIV)

A s you think of the word *process*, you might initially think of it as a series of events leading up to a big anticipated moment, or you might picture it as different levels that you have to climb through to reach a certain peak. Although we can never fully know what to expect during the process in pursuit of the peak point, we must understand that there might come a time when the journey will be frustrating. Certain stages might not be comprehensible right away; some will be very long and exhausting; others might be extremely challenging. In the end, though, there are critical lessons we must learn to be prepared for our future.

You might wonder, *Well, how do I know when I have officially begun my process? How do I know when my time has come?* It came when you experienced a storm in your life. It might have been earlier in your life, even at a very young age, or it could be right now that your process has begun. Maybe it was when you were a child and that man you looked up to as a father figure—whether an uncle, big brother, cousin, or that man that was always just around—who did some unusual things to you. He would always look at you a certain way. He would say things to you that seemed weird, such as, "You so fine, only if you were my age," or "Don't be wearing those little shorts around me." You blew it off, however, because you were too young to catch where he was going with that. Then one day he sneaked into your bedroom and began touching you inappropriately while everyone else in the house was asleep. He led you to believe that it was good for you by telling you it would make you feel better. Perhaps he threatened to kill you or another family member if you screamed or said anything to anyone about it.

Or maybe you were that teenage girl who missed your period and couldn't figure out why you kept throwing up almost every morning. You went to the school nurse for her to check your temperature to see if you were coming down with a case of the flu, but it wasn't that. The nurse informed you, "Honey, it looks like you are pregnant."

"Pregnant?!"

There is no way in the world you at such a young age can raise a child. How in the world can you explain this to your family? You knew that they were going to make you feel miserable about it, and you were afraid of their response, so, without hesitation, you got an abortion without anybody knowing. That fact you aborted an innocent life has been a struggle for you every day.

Or what about that abusive relationship you're in that has you scared for your life? He repeatedly beats you, sometimes uncontrollably, for no apparent reason. Maybe there was a time he left you on the floor, bruised and bloody. You screamed and cried *"Hellllppppp!!!"* but nobody came to your rescue.

For many years, you had no idea why something so detrimental would happen to someone like you. The only question you seemed able to ask is, *But why?* You didn't have all the answers, probably because you were too young to try and piece it all together; it left you with a bunch of unanswered clues.

Now, here you are at a place in your life when you are trying to figure out the next step. How do you continue this journey called *life*? How do you accept the process with all that it entails? How do you gain enough physical and mental strength to bounce back from some of the challenges that you might have faced along the way? Are you searching for the courage to pull yourself through some of the most life-threatening situations, or are you going to continue to lie there and let life defeat you? Sometimes the answers to those questions are in your process. You realize how strong you are when you say, *Enough is enough!* Author Gayle Forman said it best in her book *Just One Day*: "I don't know who I am. Or maybe I do know who I am, I just don't want to be her anymore."

The Uncertainty of Self

Take a good look at yourself. What do you see? Do you see happiness, or do you see sadness? Do you see beautiful, or do you see ugly? Do you see confidence, or do you see uncertainty? Do you see love, or do you see hate? Do you see weak, or do you see strong? Do you see fear or do you see faith? Do you see a girl, or do you see a woman?

As for me . . . every day I woke up, I saw a girl who felt hopeless. I felt there was no hope because I believed I would always remain the girl who was unsure of herself. I never saw me coming out of the life stage of insecurity and to a place of self-confidence. But what was confidence? I didn't know what that meant. I remember having moments where I would just stand in front of my mirror in absolute disgust at how I looked. I spoke negatively to myself all the time. *I hate the way that I look. How come I don't look like her? I'm so ugly. Nobody likes me.*

For a second, I really started believing what I was speaking over my own life. Comparing myself to other girls was the norm for me. I looked at my outer appearance and felt like I was not "it" because I had big rounded eyes, and other girls had small eyes. My teeth were crooked, and others had straight teeth. My hair was thick and brittle, and others had straight and silky hair. I was super skinny, and others had curves filling out their jeans. I had extremely sensitive skin and, well, others didn't seem to have that problem.

What did I see? I didn't see happiness; that's because I spent many nights feeling sad and alone. I didn't see beautiful, because I felt extremely ugly. Although people would tell me from time to time, "You are so beautiful; I just love your little dimple," in my mind I was thinking, *Really? So, you just gone lie to me like this?* Since it seemed nobody ever paid any attention to me, I had to create a master plan on how I was going to change that. I did everything from changing the way I dressed, to changing the way I talked, to changing the people with whom I hung around—all for some attention. Yet, all I did was fail! I had absolutely no idea of who I was or what I was trying to become.

I thought I needed to look like the image of other girls around me—how I needed to dress and what I needed to become just to get noticed, and that ultimately led me into that place of uncertainty. You want to know what that place feels like? It's a place where you begin to question your potential. It's a place where you look at your physical appearance and conclude that you will never be "it." It's a place where you begin to ask, "Do I even deserve to be alive?" It's the place where outsiders judge you and make you feel bad for wanting to have a little bit of fun, but because of where you come from and who you are connected to, there are certain restrictions that limit you from doing what you see other folks doing. My restriction was being a Preacher's Kid! It wasn't that I hated being a preacher's kid, but sometimes I couldn't deal with the platform and the image that I struggled to uphold. I never asked for it! But it was all in God's plans. He knew that it would one day be a part of my story.

The Church Girl

I have always been considered different for as long as I can remember. From my upbringing, to my family, to my surroundings, my *life* always separated me from my peers. I would hear things like, "You're special, you have a gift, you have so much anointing, you're unique, and you're *different*," but I never realized those words were just seeds being planted in me as a young girl. There were many things in my life that I didn't ask for; God just sort of knew I needed it, and I had no choice but to deal with it.

One of those needs was my growing up as a Preacher's Kid. *"What you doing here, Church Girl? You know you not supposed to be doing that, because your dad is a pastor."* I would always cry and feel ashamed when people would call me Church Girl or bring up the fact that my dad was a pastor. I didn't understand what people meant by that. I was just a regular person! I had every desire to live what I thought was a normal life, based on what I had been observing around me. Apparently, my life just wasn't a great fit with the lives of others. I assumed that I was being classified primarily because of who my parents were, and that mostly came from my classmates. The only way that I was able to get over it was to laugh it off and go about my day. I wanted so badly to find acceptance at school. I did everything I could just to be accepted and fit in,; I wanted this place to feel like a place where I belonged. I would do *anything*, give up *everything*, just to be accepted!

But God wouldn't allow it to happen that way . . . .

School Pains

My entire middle school experience and part of high school were like a living nightmare. I thought that bullying only existed on television, until I became a victim. My seventh- and eighth-grade years were the absolute *worst*! I got talked about and picked on just about every single day . . . by boys! I would hear jokes about my body size being too small, my edges being too nappy, my eyes being super big, and my teeth all over the place. People would joke on me in front of the entire class as everyone would be laughing at some of the most horrendous jokes that were made.

I would hear jokes about my body size being too small, my edges being too nappy, my eyes being super big, and my teeth all over the place.

There was a time when I told a secret about someone else's personal business to some boy I trusted not to pass on the information I shared with him, and he made me pay him to keep quiet. I'm talking like thirty dollars. Come to find out, he shared the information with others anyway. When the next person found out, that person made me pay them to keep quiet. By the time it had gotten around practically to the entire school, I was out of money. I spent well over a hundred dollars to make people promise not to say anything, when all they wanted out of it was the money.

Talk about humiliating! Talk about a living nightmare! Talk about torture! I never imagined that at such a young age I would be a victim of bullying. You think bullying is done when someone beats you up, takes your money, and runs, but bullying is done in many different forms. There is cyber bulling, which I experienced a little of; there is verbal bullying, which I experienced a whole lot of; and there is physical bullying, which I never experienced, but I totally disapprove of.

I was just a little girl. I didn't know how to handle being bullied and picked on. I would either laugh it off just to keep myself from crying or say horrible things back, which made their comeback hurt ten times worse. During those years I suffered from low self-esteem for a long time because of the comments directed at me about my physical features. I was already having a hard time with how I looked at myself, and the comments made at school to me only made it worse. Those boys made me feel like I was nothing.

I started to believe them when they said things like "You are so ugly" or "You look like a man" because I had hair on the top of my lip, even though my dad told me every single day since I was a little girl that I was beautiful. I never told my family about this abuse until I got older because I had learned how to deal with it. I didn't understand why such things like that would happen to me—I went out of my way to be nice to everybody, but I started to see that people were taking advantage of my kindness, so I had to figure a way to conquer middle school. I figured that maybe if I conducted myself in ways like all the other girls, somebody would finally notice me. I assumed that the jokes would stop. Fighting, cussing, wearing tight clothes, having my hair a certain way. Being the real me wasn't cutting it, so I had to create an image to cover up and hide who I really was.

I began to study the different types of behavior and how receptive the other students were. I'm talking the kind of behavior that gets you kicked out of class, like trying to be the "class clown"; yeah, that was me. . . . It became a constant battle for me trying to portray myself as something I was *not*. I failed big time! I would always think, *What would my parents have to say if they saw me this way?* Yet that didn't stop me. I would lock my door and stand in front of the mirror in my bedroom rehearsing different slang, cuss words, and languages that I had developed all by watching and listening to my classmates just to be sure I didn't sound too crazy.

Sometimes I can't believe I went the extra mile in doing all of this, but when you don't know who you are or what you want to be, you find yourself trying and experimenting with everything you can think of. I even tried to get away with wearing inappropriate clothing to school. It was the first day of school, either my freshman or sophomore year in high school, and I was sure that I was going to school in this romper (shorts) that came up to my butt, literally, with spaghetti straps.

As I got ready to leave the house, my father took one good look at me up and down, and he had this *Oh, you gotta be kidding me* look on his face. He told me I wasn't going anywhere dressed like that. He made me go up to my room and change my clothes into something more appropriate. I was so angry. I didn't see anything wrong with what I had on, until I stopped and remembered who my father was—the pastor. I had to remember that my parents raised me differently. That kind of attire had never been appropriate in my household; combine that with my father being the overprotective dad, and it was clear that what I was wearing was definitely unacceptable. *I knew that!* To be honest, I just wanted to see if I would get away with it for once.

I just couldn't get the hang of it. I was frustrated and angry; my master plan kept falling through. I would create a new plan, practice it, and master it, only to then have to turn around and sweep up the pieces after everything came crashing down. Here I was, a little girl at age fourteen trying to pretend to be something that I was not, just so I could fit in and act like I had it all together. But what's crazy is . . . *I didn't have it all together!* I was struggling, y'all. I wanted peace, but I didn't know where to get it from. At one point, going home wasn't even peaceful because the moment that I stepped through the door, I was walking into dysfunction!

Dysfunctional yet Functional

How is it that going home isn't peaceful? Is that even possible? Let me tell you, it can happen, and it is possible. I thought home was supposed to be a place of serenity, a place of refuge you look forward to going to after a rough day; but in some instances, that might not always be the case.

It was a Sunday afternoon, and my family and I had just gotten home from church. Because my parents were the church pastors, we were always some of the last few to leave after the service was over. On this particular day, I had been anticipating my mom's Sunday dinner—she promised to make us one of our favorite meals: pork chops and rice with sugar, with some veggies on the side . . . mmmmm, that was my favorite.

There was something different about this specific Sunday, though. It was almost like I could feel something was getting ready to happen. It was a very quiet drive on our way home from church. That's unusual for the Cohen family. I knew where this was going because I had seen this episode before. Normally, we would talk about how the service went, singing or laughing and cracking jokes, but not this time. It was dead silent. We finally arrived at the house, and not a single word was spoken as we got out of the car. I entered the house and continued to walk toward the back of the house, where my bedroom was. Before I could even change into something comfortable, I heard my parents going at it, back and forth arguing, yelling, and screaming at each other.

"I'm not going to do this with you! Get out of my face! You're not even trying to listen to what I have to say. You need to just shut up!"

With both parents trying to voice their opinion on whatever topic they were discussing, the argument got louder and more intense. Things were being slammed on countertops because of the anger and the frustration of one parent not understanding the other. At moments like that, the tone of the conversation was always distinct by its inclusion of yelling and screaming, perhaps even followed by crying. *"Stopppp!"* I screamed as I broke down and fell to the floor with tears streaming down my face. I just couldn't take it anymore. I was fed up and I had enough!

Instantly, as they heard me crying and my loud scream travelled to the kitchen area where they were, the argument ended, and my family came rushing back toward my bedroom. "Tay, what is wrong with you? Why are you crying? What happened?" But I had absolutely no words. The moment that I tried to open my mouth and speak, I just cried even harder. I lay there on the floor with my face tucked into my knees, tears gushing down my cheeks and onto my blouse. My brother and my father had to pick me up off the ground to sit me on the edge of my bed; I didn't have enough strength to get up by myself. In that moment, they began asking me questions to figure out what was going on with me, yet I had absolutely no answer. It was like something was squeezing my mouth shut because each time that I tried to open up and say something, I couldn't speak.

It was interesting to me because I had always heard about kids my age, especially, having mental breakdowns because of things that were happening in their lives, such as a loved one's death, family issues, or social-adjustment challenges, but I didn't have a full understanding of what exactly that meant until it happened to me. For the first time in my life, I experienced a mental breakdown. For many years, especially in high school, I learned how to deal with this pain in silence. I was always good at ignoring the moment when my parents would fuss at each other because it seemed as though it would happen almost every other week.

Some parents have no clue of the impact and the effect that marital strife and arguments have on the children who are living in the household and what it does to them mentally.

Some parents have no clue of the impact and the effect that marital strife and arguments have on the children who are living in the household and what it does to them mentally. E. Mark Cummings and Patrick Davies, professors of psychology at the University of Notre Dame and University of Rochester, respectively, pointed out in their book *Marital Conflict and Children: An Emotional Security Perspective* that when parents repeatedly use hostile strategies toward each other, some children can become distraught, stressed, anxious, and hopeless. Other such children tend to react outwardly with anger, becoming aggressive and developing behavioral problems at home or at school. Davies also said that children can develop sleep disturbances and health problems such as headaches. This level of stress can interfere with the child's ability to pay attention, and it can create learning and academic problems at school.[1]

I can vouch from personal experience that everything discussed from that portion of the book is true; it is relatable, and I understand the damage that emotional stress can have on a child's mind. Imagine waking up at 5 A.M., hearing your parents arguing back and forth, and not being able to go back to sleep. Then you must get up in the next few hours and get ready for school. With all that you have seen and heard on your mind, it becomes difficult trying to function throughout the day, only to come back home and have it take place all over again.

I always felt like the middle man. Most of the time, I was the one that both parents would cling to when things were rough. A lot of information had been shared with me from both sides; it left me feeling like I had to pick and choose whose story I was going to believe. It became frustrating at times because you never want to be in a position where you feel like you must pick a side, especially when you are only fourteen years old and trying to figure out *What do I need to do?* Fact is, that is not your responsibility.

I was so pro-parents and knew I needed to be there for both of them, I always tried to figure out what I could do to help their marriage. My siblings and I saw and knew too much of what was going on, and it affected us. Too much information was shared with us that we truly didn't need to know about. I've always felt like the weight carrier because I would always try to find a solution or take on their personal problems as my own. It took me a long time to get to the point where I showed little to no emotion toward the arguments and the chaos because I didn't know how to cope very well. I would always cry anytime it happened, until one day

I realized that my tears were not helping the situation, only hurting me even more.

It was different the time that I had a mental breakdown. I needed that moment to just scream and let it all out. I had so much bottled inside of me between my horrible experiences at school and my identity crisis, to my struggling with low self-esteem and suicidal thoughts; at times, I felt I wanted to just go ahead and end my life. I couldn't take it anymore. I spent many nights contemplating how I was going to do it. Would I just slit my wrist with the sharpest knife that I could find, or was I going to overdose on some medication in the medicine cabinet? I had been keeping so much bottled in that at any given moment I was going to explode!

I never understood why God allowed me to carry all that weight. Why was it that I was the first person my parents would run to when they needed to vent? Could it be that I was going to have to be the weight carrier when I got older, so God was preparing and developing me at a young age? It was rare that I would ever talk about my family's issues to anyone, even some close friends, unless it was to my older brother or my sister. I was always afraid of what people would think of me, given the fact that my parents were leaders of a well-known church in our city and they were having marital challenges. I was more embarrassed by the fact that we had major family issues because the community viewed us at this ideal "Perfect Family" that does everything the right way. I believe they didn't think that we had arguments, issues, or even struggles.

For a long time, our home was dysfunctional, yet we found a way to continue to be functional. Let me be fully transparent. There were many moments of absolute silence around the house when nobody was speaking to each other. I would come home and lock myself in my room until it was time for me to come out and eat. I experienced many nights of waking up at 3:00 A.M. to my sister running into my room crying because Mom and Dad were back at it again. I would just grab her and cover her up as we rolled over and went back to sleep.

There were moments when I would try and be the peacemaker by intervening, doing everything that I could to make it all stop . . . but most of the time that didn't help. As I got older, I became very good at keeping my personal life hidden. I learned how to make it look easy, when in fact this was the cut that hurt the most. In front of the congregation, my parents would demonstrate love and support toward each other, but behind closed doors, things were hanging on by a thread. Yes! That was us, the first family! Understand one thing: preacher's kid or not, there is no such thing as a perfect family—not for me, not for you, and not for the most popular boy or girl in school. We are all human; at the end of the day, we all have challenges with a resolution still in the distance. For many years, I believed that my family was the only family that suffered from dysfunction and other psychological challenges. Then, as I began to open up to other people and share my testimony, I found that there were more individuals than I had thought who dealt with some of the same problems.

Questions that *Need* Answers!

As a teenager, I had a lot of questions that needed answers. It's common to have questions as a teenager, because you are just figuring out this thing called life, yet on a less-complex level. The biggest question I had was why it seemed as though ministry was more important than our family. A lot of the disputes within our family (especially my parents) were primarily ministry-related. I understood that there were certain areas in ministry open to disagreement, but how did we let the toll of ministry bring us to the point where there was dead silence around the house? Why didn't we just leave ministry at the door and focus more on reconstructing what was seemingly being torn apart? Sometimes, I felt like we were in competition with the ministry. Seriously! And it would be in those moments when I felt that ministry started to pull my father away from our family.

I'm going to just be real with you. *I hated it!* I watched numerous times how my father would come home physically and mentally drained because of all the work that he had to deal with in the ministry. Not because he wanted to drain himself out, but because there was a lack of support from individuals to help him carry the weight of his vision. My father was a hard worker, and he participated in many positive acts throughout the city. He was big on giving back and ensuring that whatever is done that it be done in excellence! And that's one thing that I truly admired about his leadership. Even today wherever I go and if I am speaking in front of important people, I always explain how, from the time I was a young girl, my father instilled in me and my siblings that whatever God allows us to do, that it be done right and that it be done in excellence!

But, there were a lot of conversations he wouldn't share with us simply because he didn't want to put that load on us. Instead, he tried his best to shoulder it all himself. As a result, he would come home feeling totally tapped out. The load of the ministry would sometimes lead to his taking out his frustration and anger on us, knowing that these had nothing to do with us. I've seen so much time and sacrifice on his part, day in and day out, dedicated to the ministry, while our own home was falling apart. We would chase after these members who were leaving our church and try to figure out what went wrong instead of trying to fix the broken pieces that scattered in our private home. I had moments to myself where I would say, "I want my Dad back because I don't know who this person is." I knew that ministry was a full-time job, but I didn't think there would ever come a time where I would watch it become so draining.

We were so clever at creating this pristine image, but eventually people started catching on. We couldn't hide it anymore. People started to become curious and began asking questions, especially when for weeks my mom wouldn't show up for Sunday service. "Where's your mom?" "Is everything okay? Let her know that I'm praying for her." We hid our true emotions and our feelings as we struggled trying to keep a smile on our faces. This was to cover up our pain because we couldn't show or tell them how we were breaking down as a family inside.

As much as I loved my church and enjoyed being involved in ministry, I wanted—badly—to stop pretending and start living! I wanted to stop faking it like I had it all together; I desired to start living my life for *me*! I was more than just "the Church Girl." I needed to be free from the dysfunctional chaos inside my household. In fact, I wanted to run away from all the people who played major roles in my low self-esteem.

I had my own mindset; I had my own personality. I had my own desires, and I even had my own likes and dislikes— yet nobody understood that. There were times when I felt like I had absolutely no one to talk to; not even my family. It was very challenging because I believed no one could relate to some of my emotions, unless you had grown up a preacher's kid—then perhaps you could relate. I needed to find my way out . . . and *fast*! The more that I became anxious to want to leave that environment, the more people started to become more comfortable in making their negative comments toward me. I was being attacked, and this was by people from whom I least expected this treatment.

The Strength to Close Your Mouth!

One Sunday service, a woman who was a prayer leader at the church approached me after service to tell me that I danced very well. (Dance for me has always been a passion since I was a young girl. It's a way that I communicate with God, and it's in that place where I find answers and receive what I need. It's a safe place!)

She went on to tell me that I should not have worn my dark-colored lipstick because she thought it "too distracting." She said she lost focus of the dance because of my distracting lipstick color. She tried her best to say it in a graceful way, but I was apathetic to what she was saying. I looked at her like I couldn't believe what was coming out of her mouth. How do you respond to something like that? Do you say thank you or do you simply walk away? Do I go off on this lady and say what's really on my mind, or do I keep my composure because I have to be sensitive to the feelings of the saints in the church (because you don't want to be the reason they leave)? But what about my feelings? In that moment, God had to give me the strength to close my mouth and not lash back at the woman, although I really wanted to. I know some of you hot-tempered young ladies don't have the strength yet to do that, but there will come a moment in your life when God will allow a situation to "happen," and he will forcefully close your mouth for a reason, because if you speak too soon, it could ultimately disrupt that teaching moment.

I couldn't believe that my place of escape and freedom that day with the lady in church became a judgment zone. What's even more insane is that this was not the first time negative words had been directed toward me about my dancing (or at least my makeup for dancing). All those times, God never allowed me to say anything mean back. He never gave me the strength to type a mean and ugly message to a young woman who expressed to me via text message how envious and jealous she was of me for a very long time. I had absolutely no clue as to why she felt this way toward me.

Later on, I discovered, I just had to accept the fact that not everyone will support or appreciate my special gift, and that it is OK. The most important takeaway I've learned is that if you can't control a situation, you can control your response. I couldn't control the church lady's response or her opinion on my lip color and the dance, but I had the ability to control my reaction to her remarks. In that moment, my flesh was weak, and I needed God's spirit to work in me so that I wouldn't say anything out of order, so God shut my mouth! Of course, it took me years to figure that it was for a teaching moment, but what I realized was that this lady's emotional reaction toward me and her remarks were way deeper than my colored lipstick. It was something personal that she was battling over which I had no control or involvement. I just got fed up!

I got *sick* of being called "the Church Girl" or only being acknowledged if someone mentioned my mother's or my father's name. I wanted people to understand that I am ME! I am my own person, and I was not who God called my parents to be; I was just a part of the bloodline. From the beginning, I wanted to live what I thought was a fun, honest, and normal life; yes, I loved church, and, yes, I love everything about God, but I didn't feel normal.

My life didn't feel normal. I was always under the impression that people were watching. They were watching to see if I slipped up; they were watching to see my reactions; they were watching to see what I was doing when my parents weren't around, and it made me so uncomfortable to the point where I started doing things against my nature. Every day was like living on pins and needles, and I got sick of that. I didn't care anymore. I wanted to live my life for me and not anybody else.

"Who cares what they have to say? This is my life," so I started doing what I wanted for me! "So, you know what . . . from now on, just call me 'The Girl.'"

2
The Girl

"For I know the plans I have for you," says the Lord.
*"They are plans for good and not for disaster,
to give you a future and a hope."*

— JEREMIAH 29:11 (NEW LIVING TRANSLATION)

"T-----Is for Tennessee, S----State, U---University, TSU . . . "

THE LAND OF GOLDEN SUNSHINE IS WHAT THEY CALL IT, EXCEPT the sun wasn't always so Golden in this season. To describe this experience in four words, I would use Excitement, Experience, Exposure, and Escape. Sometimes I wish that someone would have warned me about what was headed my way, but at some point, I was going to have to find out for myself. The college girl finally arrived at her *new* school, better yet, her new home . . . Tennessee State University in Nashville, Tennessee.

I was now away from home, all by myself, finally with the freedom to be me. Oh, I was loving it! As a college freshman, I knew that I was getting ready to embark on a journey that I had deeply desired since high school.

Excitement! I decided that I was going to do whatever it took for me to live a normal life. This was a new place for me; nobody knew who I was. I was living in a different state, so I had the freedom to do what I wanted to do without having to look over my shoulder to see who's watching. The boys down South tell you that you are "it" . . . well, at least that's what they lead you to believe. A number of college upperclassmen warned me to be careful of dudes with dreads and Timberland boots, because they were all crazy. Others explained to me how I would most likely meet my husband while in college. I was so amped about dating. I gave a chance to anybody I thought was cute to get to know me. *Bad idea!*

I remember driving down Interstate 24 toward Clarksville in my beige 2001 Nissan Altima. My purse was in the front seat and my overnight bag in the backseat, and I was just praying during the entire forty-five-minute drive that my car was going to make it. I was on my way to see this guy who was a star basketball player at the time for Austin Peay University. He was a preacher's kid like me, so instantly I felt there was a strong connection.

The first time he invited me to his game, something in me told me that he was the one. He not only bought me a teddy bear, balloon, and a card after his basketball game, but he also had tickets reserved for about five of my friends. I was so excited to see him this day. When I arrived, I got a chance to see him practice. I was mesmerized and kept telling myself, *He's definitely the one.* I figured that I had a chance to become a basketball wife, but the moment that he got around his teammates and some of his other friends, he began to show his true colors. I would hear him from time to time say little things here and there that were insulting and disrespectful. I knew that wasn't going to last any longer than it did. Thank

God, I had the opportunity to leave before things with him got too serious.

But then things started to get a little deeper . . . *alcohol.* Let me just tell you, turning down a bottle was not an option for me. I would holler across the room to my friends to pass me the bottle of alcohol while we were getting dressed, doing our hair and makeup, and preparing to go out to the club that night. Throughout my first couple years in college, I had been exposed to so much alcohol that it was consuming me. It became a lifestyle habit. I had to be drunk for me to have a good time. I hated the taste and at times even the smell. I hated how I felt the next morning—being sick, throwing up, and pretty much unable to get out of bed. However, I was madly in love with the way that it would cause me to demonstrate unusual behavior.

Just about every weekend I was at some party, club, or get-together completely drunk. There were very few nights when I could remember being sober. There had been a few nights when I didn't even remember how I got home. There was one night when I passed out after being on a party bus; three boys had to carry me home and put me in my bed.

I woke up the next day and my pants were off, yet I had no clue as to what had happened. I couldn't remember a thing from that night! I'm talking *that* drunk. Did I ever stop to think how dangerous this was to my life? How something could have happened to me? I could have been raped, molested, or assaulted. Perhaps that was not factored in because of my continued drinking. Some of you might know how hangovers feel the next morning—like *crap*! I felt like that each time, and I would repeatedly tell myself that I was done drinking, until a bottle was put in my face; and there I was again back in the same cycle.

You might wonder, what my purpose was behind all of this. Did I choose to drink because I was peer pressured into doing it? Did I choose to drink because of some internal pain from which I was trying to escape? Or did I choose to drink because I had adjusted to this lifestyle habit so completely that it became challenging for me to detach? The answer is, all of them! Drinking and getting drunk was a coping mechanism for stress, depression, and the mild cases of anxiety I would experience. I didn't know how else to handle the pressure, so I looked to this substance to resolve the issue. Yet it only made it worse.

Besides the different emotions that I would periodically experience, there was no purpose why I chose to engage in this type of activity as much as I did. I did it because for so long I wanted the experience for myself! Back in high school, I would always hear stories of other people's drunken experiences and the level of fun they'd experience while under the influence. I just waited until it was the perfect opportunity for me to have my personal encounter.

Somehow the more that I continued to drink, the harder it became for me to put the bottle down. There was no putting an end to this lifestyle because it was so addicting. It was the *exposure* that got me hooked! But it was the *experience* that got my attention. Then there was weed. I was never tempted or peer pressured into trying it, primarily because I hated the smell. I saw what it did to a friend of mine in high school the first time she tried it; she began hallucinating, and that put a fear in me that has stuck with me.

I had never smoked a day in my life. I didn't know what it felt like to be high. I had never even held a blunt, but there was something about this particular Friday night, being with a group of friends that persuaded me into smoking. So, I concluded that I was going to do it. For once, I wanted to experience being high. All my friends would talk about their experience being high, and I became curious as to what my first experience would be like.

I sat squished in the back seat of a small car, jammed in among five or six others, parked in the parking lot of an apartment building, where a friend lived. I included myself in the weed rotation. Prior to that, I paid five dollars to my friend who was also smoking with us that night for the weed that she bought because I wanted to make sure that I was able to smoke the blunt a few times. As the blunt made its way around the car to me, I took my first inhale and exhale, coughing extremely hard because of the tough smoke going down my throat. It made it difficult for me to stand the weed.

As I sat back, I could feel myself beginning to get lightheaded. With my sight starting to fade, the smell of the weed getting stronger, and the temperature inside the car getting hotter, I glanced over to my right near the passenger window. I saw a very tall and slim girl standing there. She looked familiar, but I couldn't make her out because things were looking blurry.

"Taylor? Really? Since when?!" It was my best friend shouting at me as I again put the blunt to my mouth, laughing and coughing at the same time as I inhaled. "Since today," I responded to her as I leaned back and closed my eyes.

Hers was the only voice playing in the back of my head each time I put the blunt to my mouth. By the time I had had four hits of the blunt, I was extremely high, almost to the point where I literally felt like I had blown my brains out. Immediately as I took my last inhale, I suddenly felt absolutely nothing! Instantly, I stepped out of the car, panicking and freaking out because my body didn't feel right. I was having the same experience that I had witnessed a friend back in high school having, and now it was happening to me. *What is happening to me? What have I done?* I just knew I was high. What makes this story even crazier was earlier, while we were all walking to the car to go smoke, I saw all this playing out right in front of me, before it actually happened—a déjà vu moment.

All my friends in the car began laughing at me because I was hallucinating, seeing things, running in the bushes, and calling on God at the same time to take the high away. I remember crying, "God, I promise I will never do this again. Please just take this away." What they didn't know was that I was seriously scared for my life. I felt like I was dying. I was pacing back and forth in the middle of the street because I wanted it all to go away . . . *now!*

I couldn't feel my body move, nor could I feel my feet touching the ground. It was like I was floating. My fear with weed was the day that somebody would happen to lace the weed with something bad, and I'd never be able to bounce back from it. I've heard the stories!

One thing is for certain: since that *experience*, I have never put another blunt to my mouth. Looking back, I believe that God made me *experience* weed in such a way that I would never be drawn to it again. He had to show me that although folks around me enjoy this kind of lifestyle, it was not going to be *my* story! But . . . that still wasn't enough for me.

Then came *sex*. I had made up my mind that I was never going to do it until I was married, no matter what kind of heated situation I was in. I promised myself that I didn't care what happened to me, that was something that I was standing on and nothing was going to get in the way of that commitment. Until someone *did* get in the way. I got involved in a relationship filled with manipulation, lies, and *lust*. This was the relationship that forced me to go against my beliefs, my morals, my values, and everything about my womanhood. This was the relationship that did everything in its power to strip away and destroy everything from a young girl—all for the sake of some guy's satisfaction.

I was a college sophomore, and this was my first real relationship, so I was new to this. He introduced me to so many things for which I was not ready. For some reason, I was always attracted to basketball players. They all told me that someday they would make it to the NBA, and that they would put a nice ring on my finger. Of course, the naive me back in the day believed it.

Sadly, I believed everything about his character and what he said until he started showing me his true self. That person that was hiding behind those fancy clothes and shoes was just waiting for the perfect opportunity to reveal himself to me. In the beginning, he started off as this nice, interested, sweet, and respectful kind of guy. As he started to get comfortable with me, though, his whole persona changed. He started lying to and manipulating me. His verbiage toward me changed. He started testing me to see what he could get away with, such as cussing at me and disrespecting me. He would say mean and hurtful things, such as, "You're crazy" or "I can't stand you." I would hear things like, "I'm not about to keep wasting condoms . . . either we gone do it or we not!" He was furious with me because each time we got ready to have sexual intercourse and he put the condom on, immediately I would stop him. Each time was a wasted condom . . . so, of course, that sparked a fire, but I was so young and so afraid. A part of me was so eager to try it because everyone was

In the beginning, he started off as this nice, interested, sweet, and respectful kind of guy. As he started to get comfortable with me, though, his whole persona changed. He started lying to and manipulating me.

doing it, but deep down inside I wasn't ready for that yet. I was just a young virgin who had never been exposed to this kind of environment . . . *ever!* Until one day, when he got me drunk.

That one coping mechanism, the only thing that could be put in my face and I would give in, that one thing that I truly loved—was that bottle of liquor. It was used as a way to trap me into having sex with him. It worked. Buying drinks and bottles of liquor was nothing to him; he used it to wheel me into whatever trick or game he was playing. I was a young girl who had never experienced that type of pressure, nor had I ever encountered this type of person.

Willingly, in a short amount of time, I gave up everything that I had worked so hard for and what meant the most to me. The very promise that I made to God was broken. . . . I was so ashamed. I just knew God hated me, but I didn't think I'd be with someone better than whom I was with at the time, so I gave him what he wanted to begin with. My special treasure. Almost every night I was pressured into doing something for which I was not ready. I was conned into believing that if I didn't come and stay the night, every night, knowing that I had an 8 A.M. class the next morning, then we couldn't be together anymore.

Why was I over there every night to begin with? Did I stop to think about the reputation that I was creating for myself? He led me to believe that, as "his girlfriend," I was supposed to stay the night with him every night. In his eyes that was "love." In my mind, that was foolishness, but I was afraid of losing what I was deceived into believing was real love. That's why I believed it and allowed someone so demonic to have so much control over me.

He didn't physically force himself on me, but I felt verbally abused because I was constantly told in such a demanding tone what I needed to do or what I should have been doing, or what I was not doing enough of. When I backed down and disagreed with his requests, we argued heatedly and he slammed doors in my face. I was afraid that if I let this person go, I would be miserable for the rest of my life. Yet I was already miserable, so I settled in and became comfortable with the way that I was being treated. I didn't know if there was a way out, so I stayed in it and tolerated it, even while I was hurting deep inside. I wanted this pain to go away, but I didn't know if that would ever happen.

What Did I Do to Deserve This?

As a woman, young or old, you do not deserve to be treated disrespectfully in any way. Someone who feels obligated to control you because the "man" in the relationship doesn't deserve you. Most definitely, you should never feel forced to tolerate any form of disrespect. Don't ever feel bad for putting your foot down and saying *no*, even if he tries to say you are wrong or threatens to leave you. Listen to me, *Let him go!*

I wish I had had someone around to reassure me that it's okay to put your foot down and not feel bad about it. Even when I felt uncomfortable during the entire relationship, I accepted his intolerable ways because I allowed myself to be persuaded into thinking that was "love." *Wrong!* Love is never someone feeling like a higher power over you; love is never someone making demands; love is never someone manipulating others and throwing insults; love is never making yourself out to be a victim because you wouldn't do what they wanted you to do, even if it made you feel uncomfortable.

Love should never be forced. I tried to force myself to love him. I tried to convince myself that I loved him when I didn't.

After he had gotten what he wanted out of me, he didn't want to have anything to do with me. He couldn't handle my telling him what I was not going to do. I tried to change him to what I wanted him to be as this "ideal husband." The lesson here: No matter how hard you try, no matter how many times you attempt it, no matter how close you get, you cannot change a person! *Never.*

It was time for me to *escape.* I chose not to have sex anymore. That didn't work for him, so he left. I remember being at home on spring break, and I sat there in the middle of my bed staring at my phone. I was reading a two-paragraph text message of how I wasn't it for him anymore, how it wasn't going to work, and that he was done! I thought, *What did I do to deserve this?* I didn't understand what I was reading and how all this had happened within the course of about three months. Tears flowed down my face as I kept reading the message, For the first time in my life I felt empty, helpless, angry, bitter, betrayed, broken, rejected, violated, and so many other inexplicable emotions.

I was confused because I couldn't piece together how I had allowed myself to experience so much disorder and confusion in that season of my life. The thing that hurt the most was that he had gotten exactly what he wanted and left me when I finally decided I was going to take a stand for myself. That's typical with most guys who are no good. You finally get to a place in your life where you begin to take a stand for your womanhood and that's too much for them to deal with. So, they decide they want to have nothing to do with you anymore; they are ready to move on to the next girl/woman and do the same thing.

I constantly questioned, *Was God truly behind all of this? How could he ever in a million years let this happen to someone like me? How do I move on from being rejected like this?* But then he reminded me about all those seeds and words of affirmation that had been planted years earlier in the younger me before I left home: "You're *special.* You have an *anointing.* You're *different.*" Those seeds were used as a covering over my life, even before I knew what I would be faced with.

Self-Growth

I didn't understand any of what had occurred in my life, including that specific season. That was always my question, every single day for months: *But why, God? Why? Why me?* A few years later, I came to realize that during that time, I hadn't been mature enough to grasp that there was purpose behind every situation I faced. There was more that I needed to see; there was more that I needed to go through that would eventually work together to turn it all around for my good. The rejection was needed to bring me into relationship with God.

It didn't click that God orchestrated all this to happen the way that it did. I didn't think that such a loving and caring father would allow me to experience this kind of pain; but even Jesus was led into the wilderness by the Spirit to be tempted by the devil. God allowed Job, a man who was so faithful and perfect, to be broken and lose everything he had . . . all for God to receive the glory. It took my getting older and learning more to understand that not every storm is caused by Satan. Sometimes, God himself will *purposely* allow a difficult and challenging situation to happen in your life to teach you a lesson.

But, of course, it was hard for me to wrap my mind around it that way. I was so focused on my emotions, when I should have been looking at it from a different perspective, such as "What was the teaching moment behind all of this?" I didn't like the emotional, mental, or physical pain that I endured. For a long time, I believed that because of my rebellion against "the Church Girl" persona, as well as the activities consistently engaged in without trying to change my behaviors, I was being punished.

Later in life, I found out that God never intentionally punishes you, *but* he will discipline you. It says in Proverbs 3:12, "For the Lord corrects those he loves just as a father corrects a child in whom he delights." Most parents will punish their child for misbehaving in public, not doing their chores, or perhaps because they've brought home uncharacteristically bad grades. The punishment is done to teach that child a lesson, not to deliberately hurt them or try and destroy their childhood; it's so they are reminded of the consequences they might have to deal with should that same situation occur later in life. One thing's for sure, in most cases, it is always done out of love, especially when it's coming from the right kind of parent. God operates in the same manner. He doesn't punish us with anger because of our sins or because of our negative behavior; in fact, the Bible says that the Lord doesn't deal with us according to our sin. Even though he should do that and has the power to do so, he shows us his grace and his unconditional love toward us. He teaches us with some form of correction that might not always feel good. Correction should make you a better person.

My discipline came in many ways and at different times in my life. Although I didn't like how or when it happened, it grabbed my attention, and I needed the discipline to accept being taught a lesson. God loves you enough to correct you, put you in your place, and get you back on track. It does not matter how much dirt you have thrown on someone, or how much of a mess you got involved in, or how often you consistently engage in unhealthy behaviors, his love for you is unconditional—it never runs out!

Don't be alarmed by what God uses to get your attention. It's part of your growing process. Self-growth is about learning who you are as a person. It's not done by your outer appearance or your physical makeup; it's about your inner woman. Your *soul*! Self-growth is learning what is healthy and what is unhealthy for you. It's about learning from your mistakes and taking responsibility for your actions. It's about understanding which environments are the best versus which ones are the worse. It is about being aware and fully understanding the different characteristics you carry, including those that need major work. Self-growth is about taking it one step at a time!

My process was extremely slow, but, ultimately, I ended up at that place where I needed to be, and it is OK if that is the case with you. Don't try and be the first to finish or the first to get there; it's not a race. Each stage is like a trial and error. You must be able to consider what works and what doesn't so that you can avoid making the same errors.

So, like an experimenter, I went through many phases of trial and error. I felt what it was like to be disciplined for quite some time. I knew that, in him, we will always be forgiven, no matter how many times we screw up or lose our head. I figured that if I prayed to God to help fix my situation, and if I promised not to do it again and accept the correction, that I'd be forgiven, the situation would never again arise, and that it would be all over, right? Except it wasn't that easy. I tried my hardest to run and to escape, but I kept looking back. I kept looking back so much that I ended up right back at the same door from which I had tried to escape.

A Note from Tay:

Hey, Queen,

I know that you might not understand all that is happening right now. Some things you have to go through because they are preparing you for your future you. You might not be mature enough to comprehend it all. Hang in there, Sunshine. God is with you, and your future woman is counting on you to blossom. Keep shining!

Signed,
Taybrianne

3
The Breakdown of a Blind-eyed Girl

"He heals the brokenhearted and bandages their wounds."
— Psalm 147:3 New Living Translation (NLT)

3308

THERE I WAS, STANDING IN THE ROOM *AGAIN* THAT HAD BROUGHT me to the darkest, lowest point of my life. I was standing in the same room with this six-foot-two guy, a star basketball player at Tennessee State University, who had a deep accent that was very distinct. His name used to make me cringe every time I heard someone speak of him. I despised that name so much. You could be all the way across the room and hear that voice, and instantly you knew who was speaking. This guy was considered the "cool kid" by not only his teammates but also by other students who knew him very well. Everyone seemed to flock to him; all his teammates looked up to him and admired him not only as an athlete but as a person.

I'm convinced that there was a side of him that nobody knew about, except me, of course. I couldn't believe that I was in the same room with someone who, in my eyes, was a monster.

This guy and I had dated for only about three months, the worst three months of my life. Who would have thought that someone could feel miserable in a three-month relationship?? Trust me, it's possible. I lost myself!

I had no clue as to how I had fallen so deep into his trap—blind-eyed within my own relationship. I allowed him to pull out a part of me I never knew existed—a girl who became desperate, a girl who would settle for something uncomfortable only to make him feel good, while I was left feeling unhappy. As I was standing in the middle of his bedroom, my eyes began to shift and glance around the room. The door behind me was the same door that had been slammed in my face multiple times because of disagreements, which would end with my leaving to go back, furious, to my apartment. To my left was the wall against which I stood up when we were arguing back and forth about him telling me what I needed to do and not to do. Next to my foot, I saw an alcohol bottle; it reminded me of how it was used to persuade me to be a part of something for which I was truly not ready. Then there was the bed . . . the one in which I lay, on February 14, 2015, as I broke the promise that I had made to myself years earlier of waiting until I was married to have sexual intercourse.

At that very moment, millions of thoughts ran through my mind. The aroma of liquor, Ciroq to be exact, slapped me in the face as I stood there in the middle of the room. Deep down inside, I wanted to pick up the bottle and take a shot, but I knew that would not be such a good idea. I knew what this dude was up to because that's the type of person he was.

I glanced at the TV and noticed it was some love movie I'd never seen; all I remember is that the two actors were making out. *This has to be a set-up*, I thought. I couldn't believe what I was getting myself into. Something in me wanted to run out that door and back to my apartment, but I stayed. Just as I began to have enough strength to be free, temptation came along and I gave in. I couldn't believe that I was about to give in to what I was trying to be *freed* from. How did I find myself back into the danger zone? What was it that pulled me back into this place?

I couldn't back down, because if I did I was going to make a bigger fool of myself. Instead, I thought, *Let me show him what he was missing.* And then . . . it happened. We did it! This time, I let him do whatever he pleased with my body. He got what he wanted again! I lay there undressed, yet I felt simply *broken*! I remember rolling over, thinking, *What have I done?!* My body had been violated yet again, but this time . . . it was my fault. I let him do it, and I couldn't be upset with anybody but myself. Although I wanted to cry, I forced myself to hold back tears because I didn't want to look weak in front of him.

Shattered to Pieces

It was very cold when I got up the next morning (mind you, that was like three or four hours later and it was roughly around 7 A.M.). I was freezing, just as the weather was outside. I was shaking uncontrollably, with warm teardrops rolling down the side of my face as I walked back to my apartment building. I was so cold on the inside that I was struggling to walk. Trying to put one foot in front of the other was very challenging because I felt myself sinking back into "the girl" mode.

I hated being called "the Church Girl" and wanted to be seen as a normal person, but I didn't think for one second that my desires would lead me to a place like this . . . ever! I didn't think that I would step foot back into the room that destroyed me; spiritually, mentally, and physically. The emotions that had kept me locked away returned and had gotten worse. I went back to being emotional, angry, and disappointed, but this time with myself. I began making excuses for my poor decisions, such as, *I didn't like the feeling of being alone, so I gave in.* Why was it hard for me to completely let go? Did I realize that I was actually worth *more* than what I was giving into?

The problem wasn't that it was hard for me to let go, but I failed to make any attempt to position myself to be free. I repeatedly told myself that I was ready and that it was over, but my effort to change didn't match what I was declaring. I was trying to convince my friends that my connection with this guy was over, and I was truly ready to let go. I remember they sat me down and told me from the very beginning this relationship was going wrong. They told me it was evident to them that I was completely changing into someone with whom they were not familiar. Instead of listening to what they were saying and acting on it, I allowed my vulnerabilities and my weak spots to lead me back into that place of darkness. I didn't know how to escape the pull from my breakdown, so I looked to the only thing that would help me to cope in times like this, which was alcohol.

Instead of listening to what they were saying and acting on it, I allowed my vulnerabilities and my weak spots to lead me back into that place of darkness.

I figured that the more I drank, the better it would wipe away all my emotions; not realizing that being drunk is just a temporary "fix," and the moment that I returned to sober I would end up back in that place of brokenness. The worst part about that period of breakdown was that, prior to it, this guy had asked around campus about me to see if I would be one that was "easy." He wanted to see what he was dealing with and if he had the power to turn me into the girl he wanted me to be. I later found out that he reached out to some old friends and even some people who knew me very well to see if I was the kind of girl he wanted me to be. He planned and he plotted on how he was going to do it. Whatever his plan was, it worked; he got what he wanted out of me. It hurt me deeply that someone could be so cruel and remorseless to even consider doing something like that.

I crawled back into my shell of depression and experienced small anxiety attacks. I didn't know what was happening to me. All I knew was that I didn't react to internal pain and being heart-broken very well. My body started having these abnormal reactions. This was a type of reaction that I had never experienced. On top of that, I couldn't sleep, and I couldn't keep from crying. What was I going to do? What was happening to me? "*I need some immediate assistance . . .* "

911, What's Your Emergency?

My body just didn't feel right! I didn't feel like my normal self. I needed some immediate assistance because I couldn't figure out what exactly was wrong with my body. For days I kept itching and scratching uncontrollably. I thought I was having an allergic reaction, but I have no allergies. I thought maybe it was the water, but it wasn't. I thought it was something I had eaten, but I wasn't eating much. I had no clue what it was. All I knew was that I needed urgent care. I remember banging on my best friend's bedroom door around 2 A.M. to rush me to the hospital.

Boom. Boom. Boom. "Janelle please, you have to take me to the hospital. I keep itching and I can't feel my body. I can't sleep, I won't stop crying, and I have no clue what's going on with me."

We hopped into Janelle's car and headed to Tri-Star Centennial Hospital. Once we got there and I finally made it into an ER examination room, they checked my blood pressure. It was fine. My heart rate was a little fast, but still within normal range. They checked my urine and it was clear. They did blood work and said that my potassium level was a bit low, but there was nothing major that I should have been concerned about. According to the diagnoses from the doctors, I had a low iron level and they recommended that I take some medication to treat that.

One thing they couldn't check for me was the Sexually Transmitted Demons that I had contracted. For weeks leading up until the time I went to the ER, I was battling with some evil spirits. I was so emotional and would cry for no reason at all. I was mad at the world just because I was. I started procrastinating with everything. School started to become less important, and I started drinking more. I was more excited to party hard on the weekend to free my mind rather than to attend church, where I could be fed spiritually. I had such a lazy spirit! And let me just say, those evil spirits were *heavy*! It was like I could feel this, but I just didn't address it until I had no choice but to do so.

I was afraid to tell my parents about losing my virginity. I knew they would be extremely disappointed in me because they expected more from me. Granted, we all make mistakes, but I couldn't find the courage to tell them the truth. I didn't know how to explain to my father that his daughter was no longer a virgin. I couldn't explain to my mom how I wasn't smart enough to use protection the second time I had sex with this guy. I had to brace myself to call my parents and tell them the reason as to why I checked myself into the hospital. I had to prepare myself for the response and the reaction of their hearing for the first time that I made a mistake and had premarital sex.

I remember calling my mom at 2:30 A.M. while in the car to tell her that I was on my way to the ER. There was no way I could tell her why without giving her the entire story. I couldn't even tell my dad, so I left that up for my mom to do. I knew that he was not going to handle hearing that information for the very first time well at all. Not only were they both extremely disappointed in me for having sex, but they expressed their anger over my decisions and all that I had done leading up to when I checked myself into the ER. Their main concern was the possibility of my testing positive for some kind of sexually transmitted disease or being pregnant. Glory be to God that neither one was the case.

During my first two and a half years of college, I tried hiding everything from them. They would mention parties, and I said I didn't go. They mentioned drinking, and I said I didn't drink. They mentioned sex, and I said I wasn't active. I remained in denial (to them) until the day where I couldn't hide anything anymore. My mom told me the Lord had showed her that I was battling with some spirits that needed to be broken off me. I contracted those spirits because of who I allowed into me sexually, and I believed it to be true! I had exchanged ties with someone who was trying to do everything he could to turn me against my spiritual walk with Christ! God confirmed it!

Doctors and nurses cannot heal you from demonic spirits that have been contracted sexually. They can't diagnose you and tell you what your condition is. They cannot prescribe for you anti-demonic medication and say take it twice a day. Only God knows, and he has a way of showing you! The moment that he began to show me, I knew that it was time for me to be delivered from every foul spirit I had contracted. So, I prayed, and I prayed. My family began to pray, my friends began to pray, and other people began interceding for me—until the foul spirits had been released. Sexually Transmitted Demons are *real*, and they're not something to play with. You have no clue what kind of demons and spirits somebody is carrying or what's inside of them or what spirits they've contracted from someone else. You have no clue what that boy or man might be battling with on a day-to-day basis. You don't know!

Please, ladies, be careful of the choices that you make when it comes to being sexually active with men. Just because he looks good on the outside and seems to have it all together doesn't rule out that he's jacked up on the inside. Just because he claims that he gets his check-ups and has his paperwork to show you that he is disease-free does not mean he's not positive for having spirits of laziness, bitterness, anger, resentment, hatred, procrastination, manipulation, greed, or narcissism living inside of him.

Ask yourself, *Is it worth it? Is it worth giving up what is meant to be a treasure? Is it worth having premarital sex?* If you have not experienced sex yet, please save it! Save it for your husband! I promise you it will be so worth it. I am not one to judge if you've experienced it already because I have, too, but I am here to encourage you to wait! And to protect yourself. Save that special treasure for the one who is sent by God!

More Than a Conqueror

After I finally ended all ties with this guy and completely let him go, I kept finding out more information about him. I found out that he cheated on me the entire relationship, which was why he had to find a reason to break up. He had gotten the other girl pregnant, and he wasn't sure how I would react when he broke the news to me. As opposed to telling me the truth, he had to come up with an excuse why he chose to be done with me. My choosing to finally say no and standing up for myself played a part in it, but it wasn't the real reason. Through it all, God didn't let me fall in too deep. He didn't let me slip away from him.

I couldn't even be mad at this guy for cheating because I expected that from him. His approach toward women was completely backward. He didn't care if a girl was in a relationship with someone else. He felt that if he wanted her, then he could have her. I also know that if a man is disrespectful to his mother, there is no way on earth he will have respect for some random chick he claims to be his girlfriend. This was just one of many signs God showed me that I completely ignored along the way. The relationship that he had with his mother was the first sign. He would argue with her, hang up on her, put her on his phone's block list for weeks at a time, call her horrible names, and even sometimes he would tell me how much he hated her. His rage toward his mother had a lot to do with the lack of affection and attention from his mother as a young boy. I assumed that his behavior toward me would be more respectful, but it wasn't.

There is no way I would be half the woman that I am today or have a story to share with you about my life had I not experienced what I went through. There were so many times when I felt like a terrible wreck. I was trying to fight so many battles that were not even meant for me to fight. There were days where it was hard for me to even hold up my head. I gave the devil what he wanted by walking with my head down, looking and feeling like I was defeated. He got a kick out of it, I'm sure! But once I got my second wind, I reminded him that he was defeated! How did I remind him? I no longer walked with my head down all the time. I picked myself up off the ground. I wiped away my tears, and I encouraged myself a little bit every day.

You need *not* be a victim, because you are a *victor*. You do not have to be the woman that puts up with a man's foolish ways because you believe that's all you'll ever get. I tell my friends and people close to me all the time: Don't settle for anything in life. That's not just about relationships. Always strive for better, especially when you know that you deserve better. "When you know better, you do better!" my mentor would always tell me. It doesn't matter how long you've been in a relationship—manipulation, control, and deception are always unacceptable.

Ladies, we must stop enabling abnormal behavior from men because we feel that "They're all we got"! No, ma'am! Never! Never forget that a man will continue to do what you allow him to do. If you accept the disrespect, then that's all you'll ever get. If he repeatedly cheats on you and you continue to take him back, then he's going to think that he will always get away with it. If he continues to beat you and you stay with him, he will forever think that putting his hands on you is acceptable. You as a woman must stand up and take responsibilities for what you continue to allow. Get yourself some standards and keep them high!

You are responsible for how a man treats you. How? By continuing to make him comfortable in his wrongful actions. By continuing to accept his behavior toward you. When you stand up and put your foot down, one of two things will happen: either he's going to leave you because he feels uncomfortable, or he's going to take you seriously and change his behavior. Remember, you cannot change a person no matter how hard you try, but you do have the power to change what is tolerable and acceptable.

When you are sick and tired of being sick and tired, you know that something must change. There will be some things as a woman you will not tolerate anymore. I got fed up! I was tired of living in shame, guilt, and embarrassment. I was tired of all the sleepless nights, because my thoughts kept me up at night thinking about what I could have done differently. I couldn't handle my anxiety attacks. I was tired of all the many days and nights I spent alone crying, trying to put broken pieces back together. Each time I would try to pick up a broken piece that was meant to be broken and needed to be trashed for good, I would always cut myself. I knew that enough was enough. This time, I was ready to be healed. I was ready for my wounds to be stitched back up. I was ready for God to give me beauty for my ashes.

I needed to start all over again by loving and respecting the person God himself had created and not what some man tried to turn me into. I lacked the value of a true authentic relationship with God.

I was a young college girl whose life was filthy. Self-respect and self-love were not present for me. In order to change that, I had to begin within. I needed to start all over again by loving and respecting the person God himself had created and not what some man tried to turn me into. I lacked the value of a true authentic relationship with God. I was tired of faking church. I would be saved on Sundays, but throughout the week I went back to living that filthy lifestyle. I was more than broken; I felt shattered. Shattered is broken into a million pieces, and that is what I felt. It felt like everything that I worked so hard toward and every little piece on the inside had been snatched, ripped, and cracked right in front of me. But this time, I was ready to be honest about my mistakes, my past, and my struggles.

Looking back was no longer an option because I was ready to fight my way out of my pain of brokenness into my place of *freedom!* Even through the midst of all that, the Lord reminded me that I was more than a conqueror. To show others how victorious I truly was and that I had the ability to overcome this season of my life, it was time for me to remove the mask. Behind the mask was a young girl suffering daily while hiding behind insecurities, low self-esteem, and the struggle to find acceptance. I, too, struggled with low self-esteem! I lacked confidence; peer pressure took a huge toll on my life; and I got lost trying to find my identity. I wore the mask well and knew exactly when to put it on and when to take it off. I feared that the moment that I revealed who was truly hiding behind the mask, others would look at me strange; but relative to what I was expecting, I couldn't worry about other people's expressions. I desperately needed to focus on *myself*!

I *was ready*! I ran for my *life* with no intentions of ever looking back. I got out of it, and, thank God, I never returned to it, nor did I have a desire to want to go back. This time was about self-healing, and that's just what I started to do. It was great that I wanted to live my life for me, but the way in which I went about it was wrong. When I finally removed the mask and presented myself as I was, I found security in my own self, flaws and all. I learned to love me for me and respect myself as a woman first! The moments of contemplating were no more.

I stopped making excuses for those "*I can't*" moments and started declaring that *I can*! Immediately, I let go of all the turmoil that was trying to drag me back into the danger zone. In regard to where I was headed, God told me that there needed to be a release of everything that brought about destruction and dysfunction in my life. I did exactly as he said; let me just say that has probably been the best decision I have ever made. I could feel the weight being lifted off me. I knew there would come a time where I would have to share my story, but it wasn't going to happen until I got to a point in my life where I found the freedom to remove the mask and present myself as I am!

Remove the *Mask*

For years, some of you have become clever at hiding behind many masks. Today, though, you are going to put an end to that lifestyle . . . for good! This time you are going to remove the mask and then run for your life! But this time when you run, don't look back. You've been running all your life only to keep finding yourself back in the same place because you kept looking back. You've been trying to play it safe. I'm sorry, but that is not going to work anymore.

All your life you've been playing it safe. You've been hiding behind so much pain, hurt, mistakes from your past, insecurities, and embarrassments that you've become accustomed to hiding; all you know how to do is cover up—hiding within your own brokenness. Today it is time for you to come out of it! The first step in this **process** is to remove your mask and present yourself as you are! Be honest with yourself and really dissect what that root cause to your brokenness might be. For me, it was that toxic relationship, but for you it might be something different.

Brokenness is a part of life. I would be mistaken if I told you that you will *never* experience a period where you feel completely broken. God uses our brokenness so that he can receive the glory. I mean think about it—would you pray the way that you do had you not been broken? Would you be the woman you are today had you not experienced what it felt like to be broken? And if you have never felt what it feels like to be broken, sorry to break it to you, but it's coming. At some point, we all experience it! Brokenness should make you a better individual. It helps you to develop wisdom on how to deal with relationships in the future because you remember how you got to that place and this time you know what needs to be done to avoid those dead ends. Brokenness made me love the woman that I am today!

Your womanhood is so essential. After your relationship with God, who you are and what you are should be your main priorities. You should never be in a position where you are forced to sacrifice your morals, values, or beliefs for the sake of someone or something! God is your number-one priority, and then comes yourself. Your health, your well-being, and your sanity are what matters the most. Stand for who you are as a woman. We hear this saying all the time: If you stand for *nothing*, you will fall for *anything*. If you have nothing to stand on or nothing that you believe in, you will find yourself easily swayed.

Stand up for your rights as a woman—such as *respect*! But, you must first learn to respect yourself. That was my issue. I expected this guy to respect me, but how could I expect that when I didn't even respect myself? I tolerated it even when it didn't feel good. I don't care what kind of relationship you get involved in, disrespect from any individual is not acceptable. If you are in any kind of abusive relationship—whether it is physical, mental, or verbal—you need to *get out now!*

So many more women than we realize are being abused in one or more of those ways. In most cases, they are afraid to speak up. That's because their partner has put so much fear into their heart that if they say something to anyone, the threat is that the partner will either kill them or kill a family member. A lot of times, women feel like they don't have any-body to listen to them about their being in an abusive rela-tionship or who will help them get out of it without saying how stupid they are for putting up with it even though they don't know how to get out of the predicament. As a result, they stay in it and continue to get beat up and sometimes even raped every night.

I did some research on women (college girls especially) and abusive relationships. Here is what I found, sourced from the National Domestic Violence Hotline:

- 38 percent of college students say that don't know how to get help for themselves if they're a victim of dating abuse.
- 1 in 6 (16 percent) college women has been sexually abused in a dating relationship.
- Females age 18 to 24 and 25 to 34 generally experience the highest rate of intimate partner violence.[2]

Here are some more statistics, sourced from loveisrespect.org:

- Nearly 1.5 million high school students nationwide experience physical abuse from a dating partner in a single year.
- Among female victims of intimate partner violence, 94 percent of those are aged 16-19.[3]

Wow! These statistics blew my mind, especially the one about the female victims who are in high school. The college student statistics also stood out to me because it was close to home for me. I was a college student at one point, and, thank God, I never had to experience any type of sexual or domestic abuse, but you'd be surprised at the number of college students who have experienced it and how many of those never speak up about it or report it to the police. Young college girls are suffering daily and are afraid to speak up because they are under the perception that what they are going through is *love!* I assure you that it is *not* love!

If you are a victim or have been a victim, you need to know that there is help available to you, whether you are in high school or college! Get the help that you need!! There is a domestic abuse hotline that you can call at 1-800-799-SAFE (7233). If you don't feel comfortable calling, reach out to someone who is close to you that you can trust and who can help you get the necessary help to get out of the abusive relationship. If you are being shown early signs of abuse and violence from your partner, such as changes in his behavior or his approach to you, take notes and be attentive to that. Don't wait until it's too late. Find a local church to provide you some help if you have nowhere else to go and you are in a crisis situation, perhaps even on the brink of losing your life. Do not be the one who continues to deal with this because you're afraid that if you tell anyone about it, it might make the situation worse. Get yourself out of it *now* while you can. You have too much life left in you. You don't deserve the abuse, and, somewhere, there is something better waiting for you.

Also, there are some things that you must be willing to let go of completely. Be cautious of who you are allowing into your private space. All the enemy needs is a willing vessel, and, when he gets what he needs, he will use whatever he can to trap you and get you off track no matter if it's a person, place, or thing. (Read the story in Genesis about the conversation between Eve and the snake: Genesis 3:1-7) Don't go looking to fill your voids with sexual desires, attention, *lust*, and toxic environments; none of those will strengthen you—they will not fill you up nor satisfy you; instead, they will leave you *empty*.

You never want to get to a point, either out of desperation or in seeking attention, where you start looking to fill voids in your life with all the wrong things and all the wrong people, only to still feel empty. Sex, drugs, money, boyfriends, relationships, friendships—anything that you are devoting more time to than your relationship with God is an idol. Anything that replaces God is an idol. Anything that you worship more than God is a form of idolatry. God will not only supply your needs, but he also will satisfy those emotions or fill any voids if you let him.

What you need to do is to ask God, with his spirit, to fill you only with the right things in those empty spaces, closing those open gaps in your life—gaps that otherwise might cause you to drift into a space where excessive temptation resides. When you are healed, you begin to live out that life of freedom *indeed*. Wrongful things that you once had a desire to do or a bad place that you desired to be will begin to disappear. Negative words that were spoken over you will no longer break you down; instead, you will counter it by speaking *truth*! You are one step closer to a life-changing experience. You will walk into this new season that will alter and adjust every area that has been out of place. Remember this! It won't be easy, because change is rarely easy—but it is *necessary*.

Your brokenness was a part of your process. You have just hit this breakdown point in your life because your breakthrough is on its way. God took you through it because you were built for this. The enemy will always try to use adversity to derail you, but God uses it to strengthen you and build you up. Adversity is when you find out who you really are and how strong you really are. Coming out of adversity reminds you that you are more than a conqueror. It was required for you because you stand to be who you are today because of the pain you experienced in your past. God placed you in what seemed to be a dark isolation room because he was developing you. Sometimes, that might be the only place for him to get your undivided attention.

This next journey that you are getting ready to embark on is going to require some work, discipline, action, and, most importantly, for you to be all in. This is not the season to be one foot in and one foot out. . . . No, baby, if you recognize that you are ready for change and transformation, and that you are tired of waking up every single day dealing with the same ole struggles, same ole bad habits, and just straight-up mess, you must be all in!

God clearly showed me in so many ways how I was born to be different, but he had to place me on different routes to show me what I was *not* going to do and who I was *not* going to be. That is what he wants to do with you, if you let him. Embrace every challenge and every struggle; embrace your imperfections, and even those insecurities, but no not *live* in them. The mask comes off *today!* Acknowledge that you've made a long list of mistakes in the past, but never allow those mistakes to define you. I declare over your life that you will be free mentally, spiritually, and emotionally. I pray that you will no longer look back, but that you will continue pursuing the pathway toward experiencing your Redefining Moment.

Don't spend so much time reflecting and reminiscing about the past and those shoulda, coulda, woulda moments that you miss out on the blessings and opportunities that are on the road ahead of you. Enjoy this process and know that it takes time and much prayer. You must be committed every single day toward becoming a new woman, a *whole* woman. During this process, you probably will experience tough challenges. You will come across a point where it feels like you've just hit rock bottom, but you have to constantly remind yourself that there is a promise that is on the other side of this temporary pain.

Like I did, you might feel like that broken girl; but don't be that broken girl forever. At some point, you have to be ready for more! Don't be the one who's halfway in . . . be *all in*! There are some cycles in your life right now that need to be broken, but in order for that to happen, you must surrender yourself.

A Moment of Honesty:

1. Behind what mask(s) have you been consistently hiding?

   _____

   _____

2. What was that broken place like for you? How did it make you feel?

   _____

   _____

3. How much longer will you continue to live in that season where you have experienced a breakdown? Or will you do what it takes to be one step closer to your breakthrough?

   _____

   _____

   _____

A Note from Tay:

Hey, Sunshine,

You are almost there! You are so close to seeing that woman who is hidden inside. By giving over everything—your desires, your plans, your ways to the one true God who can help you through whatever struggles or challenges you might be faced with—you will see in the end that your reward will be so worth it. I promise you. Don't look at it as if you are losing. Think about what you will win . . . your future womanhood! You get to see who she really is. I know that you are going to be extremely proud of her . . . but it starts with you. Are you willing to make the sacrifices?
Keep being amazing.

Signed,
Taybrianne

4
The Total
Surrender

"I beseech you therefore, brethren, by the mercies of God,
that ye present your bodies a living sacrifice, holy, accept-
able unto God, which is your reasonable service."

— ROMANS 12:1 KING JAMES VERSION (KJV)

W HEN WE THINK ABOUT THE WORD "SURRENDER," WE OFTEN
visualize the lifting of both hands as a way to say, "I
give up; *you win.*" We think about a person giving over of
themselves into the power of another—a higher power. It
could be that you have been surrendering so much of yourself
to influences (anything that has an effect on your character,
reputation, or behavior) instead of to the one who actually deserves your surrender (God), that it might seem as though
everything that could go wrong *is* going wrong. (Think about
that for a moment.)

There were many times when I felt like I wanted to quit
even after slowly coming away from that place of brokenness. I
felt like I was never going to break away from the cycles of my
life that I had created and never walk into that place of freedom,

because I would have occasional moments where I would just break down and cry. I would think about everything that had happened to me over the course of my life and how it all started. In that moment, one of the first things that God instructed me to do was to surrender. I had always been trying to do everything on my own, acting as if I had it all under control. I had been giving away so much of my life to so many things and so many people that cared nothing about me.

I knew what *surrender* meant. I would quite often hear the word in church, but I didn't know what it looked like in practice. I knew that my surrender would mean having to make a lot of sacrifices, such as giving up friends, habits, relationships, and even environments. This was needed so I could experience the totality of freedom. Let's just say I was really afraid. I knew that after my surrender, my life was going to take a different route (for the better, that is), and I was no longer going to be in control of whatever was to happen next. In my surrender, God broke me down all the way to my knees. He took me back to that place where I had often found myself time after time when I needed his help.

I lifted my head, raised my hands, and I began to pray like I never prayed before. With tears rolling down my face, I cried out, *"Lord, here I am! Here's my heart, here's my mind, here's my soul. Please, I need you to take complete control. I've tried to do everything my own way and how I wanted it to be done, but I keep failing. I am empty, I'm unclean, I'm filthy, and I need your help. I've made a lot of mistakes in my past, done things that completely went against you, and I need you to fill me back up again. I'm tired of failing life's tests. I'm tired of quitting; I'm tired of giving in. I'm ready to keep fighting. I have surrendered my life to so much nothingness, and it is time for me to stop playing these games and give you my life, my ways, my plans . . . everything."*

That time of my life brought out a prayer in me that I didn't know even existed. I had to get back in his presence because everything in my life was a mess. There's a scripture in the Bible (Psalms 16:11) that says, "In *his* presence, there is fullness of joy." It's one of those verses that I recite to myself as a reminder that all the freedom, joy, and happiness that I need is in the presence of God. I find what I'm looking for in that special moment. I was in desperate need of peace and I knew that the only place I would get it from was right in the presence of God. It's a place of release! This is a place where you become unapologetic about what happens while you are in God's presence. Sometimes you scream, you shout, you cry, you pray . . . and maybe even for hours! Allow whatever needs to happen during that moment to happen.

It's fascinating because you don't just get a small portion, you get the entire package. There is so much peace, there is true love, there is a sound mind, there is order, and there is wisdom! That's what I needed to receive from being in his presence; and I believe you, too, can experience the same thing.

You cannot—and, I repeat, you *cannot* willing to surrender only one area of your life and not all the others, *especially* when you know deep down inside that those other areas are the parts of your life where you need true help. It is impossible! You must be willing to yield your heart, mind, and body. You cannot hold *anything* back.

So, you might ask, "What do I need to surrender first?" Your mind. What is repeated is reinforced in our minds. The more you continue to engage in unhealthy activities and find pleasure out of it, the more that you will begin to train your mind that this unhealthy behavior and lifestyle is *good* for you. What is remembered will always influence what you do. If you remember how sex made you feel, and you do this without surrendering your mind unto God and asking him to help control your thoughts, you will always find yourself—somehow, some way—drawn back into those sexual desires.

I want you to ask yourself these following questions. Be *honest* and write down your answers.

1. What kind of thoughts come up in your mind that constantly pull you away from living a better lifestyle?

_____

_____

_____

2. How much control do those thoughts have over your life?

_____

_____

Not only should your mind be part of your surrender, you also must be willing to surrender your body as well. The Bible says that we are to present our bodies as a *living* sacrifice, holy and acceptable unto God, which is our reasonable service. Everything that we do on a regular basis, whether it's sexual, how we dress, how we take care of our physical body, how we women use body language when in conversation with others, how we present ourselves generally—all should be done in such a way that we are honoring God. It's the least that we can do!

So many times, we've allowed our flesh to operate the vehicle. Then we wonder why we run into too many *stop* signs; every corner we turn, it's a dead end, and we always seem to end up in a ditch somewhere. For some of you, it might be very challenging to detach yourself from sexual desires; one might say she enjoys the pleasure so much that it has become a drug for her. Others might say that sometimes they can't seem to control their bad attitudes, which may lead to physical violence. Whatever it may be for you, I can assure you that if you want to be free from it, you can set yourself free.

Here's what you must know. If you have made a mistake in an area of your life, know that God will forgive you when you repent, and he will give you the power to *resist* temptation. That's not only with sex but also with anything that you have done that has pulled you into a place where you don't belong. *If you want it!* Temptation will come, but you cannot continue to give yourself over to those moments each time they occur. God will never tempt us to do anything that is evil; we are tempted when we are drawn away from him by our *own* desires.

Remember that with every temptation, there will always be a way of *escape*. There will always be an exit sign posted close to you so that you can *get out!* You can be released from it, but you have to be willing to surrender it all! *And avoid it!* Our problem is that we don't know how to just avoid stuff and say no! Learn the power to *just say no!* Plus, you do have the power to walk away! How many times in your past have you walked away? It is imperative to understand that a part of breaking the repeated cycles in your life includes surrendering.

From My Surrender to the *Shift*

My whole life changed once I surrendered. Old habits, desires, and ways that once had so much control over my behavior and who I was starting to become had been removed from my life. It did not happen overnight, but I could tell the difference. I got to a place where I regained my focus. In exchange, God gave me back everything that was stolen from me. Think about how your life could change if you surrendered and gave up everything to him. In those times when it felt like you were losing the fight and just wanted to quit, did you get down on your knees and say, "*God, help* me or *save* me from this mess?" How many times have you tried to do everything your own way, and it seemed like nothing was working?

Maybe you are in an unhealthy relationship right now. You have been surrendering so much of who you are to that guy who doesn't even show you that you are appreciated. He's not making any attempt to be a better man for you by helping you to grow in all aspects of your life. He's not taking an active role in helping you fulfill your destiny, and he's not holding you accountable spiritually. Yet, all he seems to be doing is giving you all these orders and trying to control your every move. You are doing all that you can to keep him around because you feel that you have the power to change him into what you want him to be. As a result, you find yourself stressed and on this emotional rollercoaster, because you have been investing so much of your time and energy in a relationship that is not even worth it.

Or those groups of friends that you might have been holding onto since forever, even though you know that they're not doing anything positive in their lives and certainly not in yours. Everyone seems to be complacent with where they are in life and accepting "just enough" to get by. No one within your circle of friends seems to be sharpening you or holding you accountable for living a better lifestyle. Iron sharpens iron. . . . Can you honestly name at least two people within your circle who sharpen you? Is there a need for surrender of your choice of friends?

Total surrender begins with asking yourself, *How bad do I want it?* "Surrender" is most commonly used as a battle term. It implies giving up all your rights to the conqueror. When one surrenders, they lay down their arms, wave a white flag, or raise their hands as a sign to the conqueror that they give up; the conqueror now has the right to take control. God, however, is the ultimate winner, and you'd better believe that he is the true conqueror.

God is with you every step of the way, but you must show him that you need his help. Let him conquer; let him be the winner in your life so that he can take complete control of it all. In the end, he is the ultimate winner.

Since that is the case, know that you are not in this alone. God is with you every step of the way, but you must show him that you need his help. Let him conquer; let him be the winner in your life so that he can take complete control of it all. In the end, he is the ultimate winner, so there is no need for you to constantly fight this battle alone. Stop assuming that you can handle it all on your own—you can't. (Let me just tell you. I've had to learn that the hard way, man, and that thing doesn't feel good at all—having to learn it the hard way! I've always been the type to say, "I'm good" or" I got this," and that I'm gonna figure it out . . . until God finally *forced* me to let him be in control of my life.)

You can surrender! You can do it! Let go of that pride and your ego and give them over to him. Give God a chance to give you a new direction and guidance toward your future. Give him a chance to strengthen you to be able to go from being the girl to the *woman*! Don't be afraid to cry out to God. I do it all the time and it is extremely healthy. Like a mother knows the distinct cry of her baby, God the Father knows your cry, too, and he can interpret your cry even when you have no words to speak. Scream or yell if you have to! Fall on your face, humble yourself, be honest with God and *repent*! Let it out. You've been holding onto this thing for too long now. You are burnt out and feel like you have no more energy left in you because you keep trying to hold on to what was meant to be dead a long time ago. It's time to let it go!

You must be willing to do whatever it takes! If you lose friends in the surrender, *so what*?! That means they weren't really your friends to begin with. If God removes you from certain places that you thought were fun and exciting, don't worry because everything that looks good to you might not always *be* good for you. You'll appreciate the shift and understand why it was necessary to be removed from certain places.

Oh, and unstable relationships . . . yeah, don't worry about those either. "*He*" probably has not *found* you yet! So be patient.

The moment that you surrender, you relinquish everything that has to do with your *self*. That includes your past, your mistakes, your struggles, your strongholds, your opinions, your own desires, and your *own* agenda—and giving all that over to the one who has the *true* power. In exchange, you receive freedom, you receive grace, and you receive peace in every area of your life. I guarantee you this; you will experience a shift in your life the moment that you totally surrender. The shift is going to happen when you are willing and obedient. It entails letting go of everything from which God has instructed you to detach.

The shift might involve a job promotion, new and healthier relationships, and even an increase in your finances. Expect the shift with your obedience to come in unexpected ways and unexpected places. Understand that surrender is hard work, no way around it. It takes much prayer, discipline, meditation, mental preparation, and physical positioning to give everything over completely. You must be in the right frame of mind to even be in position to surrender. Sometimes you must turn everything off so that you might be able to hear from God. Trying to surrender with your phone right next to you, music playing, and the TV on is going to make it much more difficult for you to hear and be attentive to the instructions that God is giving you.

Don't worry! You can do this! The surrender begins *now*! Make this moment very intentional between you and God. Continue this journey, my beautiful queen; you are one step closer. Your freedom *awaits* your surrender!

A Moment of Honesty:

1. How much of yourself have you been surrendering to bad habits, people, and places?

_____

_____

2. Are you willing to give it all up no matter what it might cost you?

_____

_____

3. When was the last time that you let out a good cry for God to help you? How did it make you feel? Are you in need of another good cry?

_____

_____

_____

4. Who can you think of right this moment in your circle of friends who is/are sharpening you?

_____

_____

_____

A Note from Tay:

Hey, Beautiful,

Stay strong and don't give up! I know it hurts right now, and you don't like feeling the pain that you are experiencing, but remember that pain is only temporary. It won't be forever, I promise! God gives the toughest battles to his strongest individuals, and you were built for this, Honey. Don't quit; keep on going!

Remember that no matter where your life takes you, always be true to yourself and don't let anyone strip you of your woman-hood. God is with you, and your future woman is counting on you to blossom.

Keep sparkling.

Signed,
Taybrianne

5

The One Who Demands *Freedom*

"Therefore, if the Son makes you free,
you shall be free indeed."

— JOHN 8:36 NEW KING JAMES VERSION (NKJV)

FOR MANY YEARS FREEDOM HAS BEEN ANXIOUSLY WAITING FOR you to open the door and let it in. It has been waiting for you all along; it was hiding because it knew that it was going to take some maturation time before you'd be willing to fully obtain it. Freedom had to watch how you navigated through life's trials. It observed the process of confusion, brokenness, pain, and even betrayal—all for you to finally come to an acknowledgment that there was a need for you to surrender. In the surrender, Freedom saw the desperation within your heart to walk away from that which was old and into the new. It came out of its hiding place after all those years because it knew that you were finally ready to be free!

Take a moment to examine who you are and where you are right now. Think about your independence. Think about all the careless decisions that you have made or are now making because you've had the freedom to do so. Think about all the times where you've had the opportunity to walk away and say *no*, but you chose not to. Think about the mess that too much of the wrong you had encountered because of freedom. **How long will you continue to stay in that place?**

When I was still living at home with my parents, I begged for freedom. I begged for them to let me hang out late at night or go to parties in the neighborhood that were not safe, or sleep over at my friend's house, and the list goes on and on. In my mind, that was true freedom. I wanted the ability to enjoy my life around people whom I wanted to be like while being able to do the same things they could. Most of the time, I had to sneak around and do things behind my parents' backs just to have fun. I was very sly and I found myself lying a lot just to do things I knew my parents would not approve of me doing.

I would have it all figured out until I started getting caught, and then I became a terrible liar. It wasn't that my parents prevented me from having fun and enjoying myself; there were just certain places that I knew even before asking I was not allowed to go. My father, especially, didn't believe in staying out late at night and sleepovers at other folks' homes. They were very protective over us growing up because they didn't always trust other people's motives.

I was the child who could never sit in the house. I always had to be doing something, and that didn't always involve safe environments. It's no wonder my parents had more restrictions on me than on my two siblings. I was the "wild child," which is why parties, sleepovers, and trying to hang out past curfew were my thing! It's crazy, now that I am older I can appreciate their having told me *no* when I wanted to go certain places or do certain things. When I finally moved out and had the opportunity to get the independence that I had been waiting for my entire life, I didn't know how to handle it. It was weird for me when I got to college not having a curfew, nobody to check in to—I could move and go when and where I pleased at the beat of my own drum. *I loved it!*

I would come into my dorm extra late, sometimes at three or four in the morning, just because I had the power to do so. I went to just about every single party just because I could. I took advantage of that freedom; as a result, it led to my making poor decisions, which eventually got out of control. It got to where I couldn't contain myself. I was making careless decisions left and right; my priorities were not in order, and that's how my life ended up a mess. It was almost as if God were saying, "Here you go; you asked for the freedom; I'm giving it to you. Now show me how you are going to manage it."

I wasn't very good at that. After experiencing all that craziness brought on by my mismanagement of the freedom and the mess that I got myself into, I needed the right kind of freedom to get me out of it. I was desperate for the true freedom. I'm talking about the kind of freedom that comes from God—that could get me out of the tangles, knots, and kinks in my jacked-up life. The freedom that would deliver me from every dark place, every place of the unknown, and every crooked pathway. *That's what I needed!*

I demanded the type of freedom where I would forever be free from erroneous relationships and unhealthy environments that would cause me to fall back into the hands of this world. Too much of the wrong freedom caused me to turn into this girl who was lost and unsure about her identity. I got so caught up in finally being able to do what I wanted to do that I found myself repeatedly making careless decisions. Don't allow your freedom to cause you to put yourself in harm's way. Learn how to manage your freedom by discerning when, where, and how to use it. There is a time and a place for everything. Just because you have the freedom to participate in foolishness doesn't mean that you must be a part of the foolishness. Learn the power of just saying *no!*

The Choice Is Yours

Who will you choose to be?

Will you be the one who finally breaks free from your past, after going through so much of what seemed to feel like hell and back, before realizing that you couldn't do it alone, so you gave it over to God. In exchange, He gave you the ability to walk in freedom, yet you are so afraid of what it might cost you. You keep one foot in and one foot out just to play it safe. You say you're ready to walk in freedom, but you are not ready for transformation because you are aware that your life will change forever. You know that you might lose some of your close friends because they truly don't understand this next phase of your life; I'm talking about these friends that you grew up with who never in a million years did you think you'd lose. There's some stuff that you are not ready to give up just yet. These are things that you really love and cherish so much but you know what God has shown you that for you to move to the next level, you must be willing to sacrifice—even some of those things that you cherish the most. This is the woman who finds herself in a place of stagnation, going back into those same cycles by keeping one foot in and one foot out. This is the "I'm just playing it safe" kind of woman.

Or perhaps, you will choose to be the woman who is totally and completely ready for that freedom *indeed.* She is the one who is confident and makes that choice that she will no longer let anything come in between her and her freedom. This woman has experienced the kind of freedom that has caused her to make terrible decisions, and now she is ready for what is right. She has done all that she could possibly do with her own human strength and figured out each time she failed that relying on herself was not a good strategy. This is *now* the woman who is willing to let everything dysfunctional and deficient go. This is the woman who is finally ready for a fresh start. This woman has both feet in because she understands that this next season of her life is going to require her to be all in, holding nothing back. This woman walks with her head up instead of down. She always has a smile on her face and is always optimistic in any situation. She knows what it felt like to always be depressed and angry, so she decides that this new woman will be the woman who lives her life for herself instead of living her life trying to please everybody. This woman doesn't care about whom she loses along the way and what sacrifices she has to make, because this is about being free indeed! This is the "I'm all in" kind of woman!

I Challenge You . . . Who Will You Stand to Be?

I challenge you to be the woman who demands freedom over your life. *Freedom* is an action word. Freedom is a lifestyle. It's not something you speak; it's something that you live by. There is evidence when you are truly free . . . in Christ! Being free does not come when you continue to hold on to that part of your past, especially when you've been told multiple times to let it go. It comes when you make a conscious decision that it's time for more. Demanding freedom over your life is when you no longer allow any person, or anything, or even a place to dictate your happiness or disrupt your peace.

Freedom happens when you stop making excuses and you just do it! Be free . . . What are you waiting for? Freedom comes when you learn to demonstrate love and forgiveness in your heart. It comes with a willingness to leave everything behind if needed to get closer to God. In Matthew chapter 19, Peter (who was one of Jesus's disciples) told Jesus that he has left behind everything just to follow him. What then will there be for us? The answer: access to freedom when you leave everything behind and with no regrets. *No regrets!*

Freedom will only come when you accept it. If you never accept freedom because of the fear of transformation and the fear of what others might have to say, then expect to always be bound.

Freedom is accepting divine love, accepting joy and happiness, accepting Christ into your life, and accepting the mistakes from your past but not living in them. Freedom is accepting who you are and living in truth! (You shall know the truth, and the truth shall make you *free.*) Freedom will only come when you accept it. If you never accept freedom because of the fear of transformation and the fear of what others might have to say, then expect to always be bound. You'd be surprised that some individuals prefer not to experience transformation because they have become so accustomed to their daily lifestyle habits and various patterns.

The thought of adapting to change is scary for some, so they'd rather live their life the same way they've been living it for the last six or seven years. That is why the lack of growth will be evident. Freedom is made available to those with a heart of willingness to surrender—a heart to give up their life to the Creator of Life and everything in it. A heart of Repentance. Your freedom is in your surrender! There is freedom in repentance. We must make sure that we are consistently asking God to fill us with his Spirit. God's word tells us that we are *to bring every thought into submission to the obedience of Christ*, which means that everything that goes on in our mind must always be submitted to God, such that whatever we might find ourselves thinking will never be higher than his knowledge.

Release and walk away! Make a strong commitment that you will break the habit of looking back. When you finally release without looking back, you experience joy, happiness, true love, peace, and forgiveness. Destroy the spirit of pride that tries to hinder you from forgiving a person for what they have done that was hurtful to you. Destroy that spirit of envy that tries to prevent love from being filled in your heart. Your heart should be filled with so much love to the point where you're loving people that you don't even know. *Why?* Because God instructs us to love even those we don't know. For even our own enemies we are to demonstrate love!

Trying to move forward will only become more difficult if you never let go of the past. Confront the root that is stopping you from being totally free and then make a *command* that it will not have control over you anymore. Freedom includes letting go so that it positions you to be able to forgive. I know . . . it's hard for us women, because we repeatedly say it about how we will never forgive and each time that we see that person we have flashbacks of what happened that was hurtful. But just pause for a moment. . . . Have you ever wondered that maybe the root cause to your lack of forgiveness toward others is because you haven't forgiven yourself?

A Moment of Honesty:

1. What is the *one* thing that is standing in the way of your being free?

2. What kind of luggage are you carrying with you on this road toward being redefined?

_____

3. Are you willing to be all the way in to experience true freedom?

_____

A Note from Tay:

Hey, Beautiful,

I just want you to know that I am proud of you. You are making so much progress. I don't want you to stop. Keep on thriving! I know it is very difficult for you to forgive that guy, those friends, or that family member for what they have done or said to you in the past, but this is about your healing. There is so much that God wants to do for you and through you, but don't let the lack of forgiveness block your next blessing. God is with you, and your future woman is counting on you.
You got this; keep thriving!

Signed,
Taybrianne

6
The One
Who *Forgives*

"Get rid of all bitterness, rage, anger, harsh words, and slander, as well as all types of evil behavior. Instead, be kind to each other, tenderhearted, forgiving one another, just as God through Christ has forgiven you."

— EPHESIANS 4:31-32 NEW LIVING TRANSLATION (NLT)

ONE OF THE HARDEST STRUGGLES IN LIFE'S JOURNEY IS FORGIVENESS. Both men and women struggle! Why do you think this is? Why is it that we are rarely taught, or open to hearing about, the importance of forgiveness, except when we are at church listening to a sermon? Or when we were young and our parents would tell us to hug and forgive a brother or sister anytime we had an argument or disagreement? What were our parents trying to instill in us at such an early age?

Of course, we never thought that it mattered because we wanted to simply be mad or be right, when in fact we were probably wrong. We don't see this as an important factor because it's rarely taught to us the greater purpose that it serves. This is a struggle especially in our millennial generation because we simply don't forgive. It is not that we don't know how to forgive; it's just so hard for us to put ourselves in position to forgive. The pride and the thought of *I don't want to look weak* cloud the mind and prevent the phrase "I forgive you" from coming out of our mouth. That's especially true when we have forgiven time and time again, and each time we remember why we don't like to forgive to begin with. What usually happens is that we wait for an apology from the person or people who have wronged us and we use that as the basis once we get that other person's apology to determine if the apology is sincere or not. Then we think that if we forgive that person, we are giving them free will to hurt us again. We don't want the person to feel like they have "earned" our forgiveness, so we are constantly going back and forth with ourselves. Eventually, we get to a point where we end up withholding forgiveness. It's one big head game.

But how can you expect to be free if you don't learn how to forgive? Forgiveness is vital. God cannot forgive you if you are walking around mad at folks for what they did to you years ago, and you don't know how to move on from it. Learn how to let it go and move on! As long as you allow unforgiveness to be bottled in your heart, true freedom will continue to be your struggle.

Some of you might need to evaluate your heart. Is your heart in a position to be able to forgive? Start by forgiving yourself. Say, "You know what? I forgive *me* for engaging in lifestyle habits that had negative effects on my behavior. I forgive *me* for thinking that I had it all together as if I could live this life on my own terms, when actually I just can't. I forgive me for those moments when I didn't look to God for wisdom and direction before allowing that man into my life who was never even designed to be with me from the beginning." When you get to that point in your life, the walk of freedom becomes so much easier. I just didn't know how to forgive myself. I kept blaming myself, I kept tearing myself down with phrases such as "How could you be so stupid . . . ?" But I realize that my speaking negative over my own life was not helping me to rebuild my self-confidence; instead, I would find myself hurting even more.

Take a moment and think about these bullet points that follow. You may write them down or answer them to yourself in your head:

- Do I realize that there is an unsolved root cause for my lack of forgiveness?

- Could it be that I have not forgiven myself for the damage that I have done?

- What about the time when I asked someone else for forgiveness and they didn't forgive me—how did that make me feel?

- Where did my lack of forgiveness begin? Who was it that caused me not to develop the heart of forgiveness?

- Have I actually tried to forgive from the heart in addition to just speaking the words "I forgive you"?

You *must* understand that forgiveness is a choice that *you* and only *you* can make! Others around you can advise you about what to do or even what to say, but at the end of the day you have to make that ultimate decision for yourself where forgiveness lies within your heart. It starts with God healing your heart. By withholding forgiveness, you are saying that it is OK for you to remain in the place of emotional bondage. You are allowing your emotions to stop you from doing what you know will bring you true freedom and total wholeness. What we don't understand is that forgiveness is not solely for the benefit of the other person; it also is for our own sake.

"In prayer there is a connection between what God does and what you do. You can't get forgiveness from God, for instance, without also forgiving others. If you refuse to do your part, you cut yourself off from God's part." (Matthew 6:14-15 MSG) It is not that God will cut you off for not forgiving others for what they've done to you, *but* he cannot do what he wants to do for you and through you (like giving you true freedom) if you are unwilling to forgive. If you want God to forgive you of your dirt, and your past, you must put aside your pride, even while it hurts, and forgive that individual for what they did to you. I am a witness! I just couldn't grab ahold of the concept of forgiveness. I was the one who thought, *Well . . . why do I have to forgive him, especially when he never apologized? He did me wrong, so why does he even deserve an ounce of forgiveness?* But all along, that bitterness and unforgiveness within my heart was eating me up every single day.

Not only that, but the lack of forgiveness and the mindset of *I'm never going to forgive* can also block blessings! I've seen it happen in my own life. Doors were shut and things came to a halt in my life because I allowed this one barrier to keep me from reaping blessings. Once I allowed God to open my heart to forgive (and not even from a place of expectancy of an apology, but simply because I needed to be healed), God immediately started opening doors. He instantly started moving in my life. I felt the new me announcing its arrival. I felt free. My prayer was not that someone would apologize to me first, but for God to fix my heart to be able to forgive that person with or without an apology.

Forgiveness for some of you might be difficult! Join the club. Trust me, I understand. Even with close family and friends who have done me wrong or said mean things to me, it was very challenging for me to forgive them! That's primarily because I didn't expect people close to me to hurt me with their words. And *yes*, words do hurt! But with much prayer and God positioning not only your heart but also your mind, forgiveness becomes easier. Forgiveness makes you stronger!

Here are a few steps that have helped me, and I believe will help you, too, on how you can position your heart to be able to forgive:

1. **Pray!** Pray that God will give you the right heart to forgive.

2. **Write.** Write down the names of all those individuals whom you have not forgiven for the internal hurt that you are still living with.

3. **Speak.** Speak it over and over to yourself that you will learn how to forgive, and you won't continue to live a life full of grudges.

4. **Do it!** Go and forgive those individuals. Watch how that weight will be lifted!

Gandhi said it best: "The weak can never forgive. Forgiveness is an attribute of the strong." Forgiveness is an act of humility. You are not weak for forgiving others, so don't let anyone try to make you feel that way. Forgiveness is a sign of strength, it's a sign of courage, and it's a sign of wisdom! Understand this is about *you* at the end of the day. This is about your healing and your freedom! Who cares if you are called weak for forgiving or are told how much you shouldn't forgive others? Typically, those types of people are the ones who are living in misery because they don't understand the power of letting go. But *you* do, so set the standard! This is about your making a choice to do what you need to do (if that is forgiveness) to experience your redefining moment.

You can do it! You can forgive. It's already in your mind; now allow God to put it in your heart. Forgive that boy for the emotional pain he caused you; however, this doesn't mean that you have to be back in a relationship with him. Forgive that family member for what they did to you when you were a little child; I know you probably hate them by now, but you have to forgive and move on! Forgive that old best friend for how he or she betrayed you and did you wrong; they didn't know any better, but you do!

Forgive yourself for any self-inflicted pain. Your freedom and forgiveness work together interchangeably. The more open you are to forgiveness, the greater your access to true freedom. You are on this journey for a reason. Everything that you are learning in life is only developing you. They say experience is the best teacher. Appreciate those experiences, learn from them, and then *grow* from them! Prayer is what held me together the whole time. When I felt like I hit the lowest point in my life, it was prayer that helped pull me back up. When I didn't know how to forgive, I looked to prayer as the answer to fixing my heart. In the midst of adversity, I learned how to develop a prayer life. Prayer is what will sustain you. Prayer is what will get you through some of the most difficult life situations. I cannot stress that enough to you. There is truly so much power in *prayer*!

Prayer Still Works

Growing up, we would hear folks—like our older aunts and uncles, grandparents, and elderly people in the church—constantly say that "Prayer still works." Why do they keep reminding us younger people that prayer still works? I think it's because we don't grasp the power that prayer has. We think that because we don't see God moving or intervening when we want him to, or that because he doesn't do what we pray for right away or operate according to our time schedule, that our prayer is ineffective! It does not mean that God doesn't hear your prayer or it's ineffective; it just means that God will move and make things happen when he feels it is necessary to do so.

*That's the beauty of our God—he knows exactly what you need, when you need it, and **HOW** you need it even before you recognize that there is a need.*

God *never* operates according to our time. His timing is always the best time! We hear things such as, "He might not come when you want him to, but he's *always* on time." That's the truth! Trust me . . . he hears your prayers! He knows what you are going to pray about even before you pray because he knows our every thought! To me, that is so fascinating! That's the beauty of our God—he knows exactly what you need, when you need it, and *how* you need it even before you recognize that there is a need.

I thank God for my family because I know that it was their prayers that covered me and helped get me through school, with my being hours away from home with no family. When the enemy tried his best to destroy me, those prayers were used to protect me from whatever plan Satan created for me. I remember I would always look to my mom or my grandma to pray me through tough situations. For some reason I felt like their prayers had more power than mine. Sometimes I wouldn't know what to say, so I would always call my mom to pray for me.

I remember one time I called my mom asking her to pray for me during a tough season, and she told me, "Mama will always be here for you, but at some point you have to learn how to pray for yourself." Those words have always stuck with me. Since then, I have learned how to pray for myself. I learned how to pray myself through difficult situations. I would have normal conversations with God about how I was feeling and what I needed his help with. The more that I continued to talk to him; the more I found comfort in praying for myself. I would begin noticing a shift in my prayers. My prayers went from five minutes to fifteen minutes. Eventually, I began talking to God throughout the day and not just before going to bed.

When I felt that nobody was around for me to talk to, I would always find a place where it was just me and him. My prayers went from normal conversations to me crying out to him with tears pouring down my face. When I had done something that I know that I should not have done, I was honest with him even when it hurt. There were times when I have seen God answer my prayers instantly, and then there were other times when I felt like I was waiting for years before my prayers were answered.

Prayer was another special key that unlocked my door to my freedom! You do not need to have all the right words to say, nor do you need to have a certain tone in your voice to pray for yourself or to pray for someone else. Prayer is a conversation between you and the Father. It is about being intimate with him! It is about your being honest with him. More importantly, it is about you listening when he speaks, because he is always speaking. He will always tell you what to do, but you must be able to discern his voice from your voice as well as those other voices around you.

Prayer is what will sustain you when you feel like giving up.

Prayer is what will push you when you feel that you have

no more strength left in your body.

Prayer is what will cause you to go from the Girl to the Redefined Woman.

Prayer is how you will be able to reach God and experience him on a whole different level.

Prayer has the power to change your situation around, and it still works!

My advice to you, even if you have never prayed before, is to write down your prayer on a piece of paper. Write out what you want to pray and then recite it every day. Recite it until you believe whatever you pray with the expectation that it will happen, if it is something that you are expecting God to do. If you write down your challenges and struggles and need God to help you overcome them, believe that it is already done, and he will be there for you. Death and Life are in the power of the tongue, so what you *speak* has the power to manifest.

Oftentimes, we spend time praying to God and complaining about all that is going wrong in our life, but it is rare that we just pause and thank him for all the good that has happened to us. For a long time that was me. My senior year in college, I spent a lot of my nights and even days complaining about everything that was going wrong. I would complain about not having enough money, or the job that I wanted, bills that kept occurring and just feeling like I was not where I wanted to be in life or where I thought that I should be in life. I found myself stressed and even depressed at times because I was always thinking about things that were out of my control.

These were situations that God would eventually work out, but because I felt the need to try and fix the situation, I found myself angry and emotional . . . a lot. Once reality kicked in, I told myself that I would show more gratitude and be thankful because my situation could have been a whole lot worse. I started praying less for myself and more for others without telling them that I had been praying for them. Instead of praying to God, telling him my needs and wants, I would thank him for what I already had. I would read scriptures that had a lot to do with being thankful and with the understanding that God already has my situation worked out. That helped to change my perspective.

Once I developed the mentality of gratitude over attitude, little by little he would give me unexpected blessings, all because of my appreciation and faithfulness over the little things. Now, I'm not saying to not tell him what you need and ask him for help, but I am saying that we must get out of the habit of only talking to him when we need or want something, or only when times are rough. You know how that feels, I'm pretty sure. That one friend or family member who calls you only when they need something but never turn around and say thank you for the time that you have helped them in the past; that crap is annoying! You have every reason to be thankful because, remember, your situation could be worse!

Power of a Praying Woman

I challenge you to be the woman within your group of friends, your relationship, on your job, in your family, or even at school that individuals look to when prayer is needed. Prayer is the foundation of a sustainable lifestyle spiritually, physically, and emotionally. Most importantly, it is vital to your relationship with God. Be the one who is not afraid to pray for someone. If it takes you outside of your comfort zone, trust me, you are in the right spot. I can't tell you how many times I have been led to pray for people in places that seemed to be strange and outside the norm. It was more so fear that kept me contemplating about praying because I was afraid of how receptive the individual I was praying for would be, but I knew that I was on an assignment, so my fears would soon fade away.

Understand that you have the power to change your situation when you begin to pray. Your prayer has the power to disrupt the plans of the enemy concerning your life. When you begin to pray, and you are so in tune with the Spirit of God, your prayers will intensify and will ultimately turn into a level of praise that makes the devil mad! Let both prayer and praise be your weapons anytime the enemy tries to come against you. Develop the mentality of gratitude rather than the habit of complaining. Watch what happens! I guarantee you, when you begin to pray, you will begin to see things change in your life. The more that you continue to pray, the more you will begin to see miracles happen in your life.

One of my favorite scriptures that I find myself reciting over and over as a reminder is Philippians 4:6: "Do not worry about anything, instead pray about everything. Tell God what you need and thank him for all that he has done."

Pray that God will continue to lead the right people into your life—people who will help to sharpen and strengthen you. Pray that God will remove any distraction that will get in the way of your transition to the Redefined Woman. (This is the season for you to remain focused.) Pray that God will continue to give you discernment over every situation that is presented to you. (This involves being able to distinguish between what will be good for you from what will be bad.)

Find time to have a private moment with God. In those private moments behind closed doors with God is where you find answers. I have spent many nights alone, on my face with the lights off, no makeup, hair pulled up, tears streaming down my face, and it's just me and God. I guarantee you that after an experience like that, you will feel refreshed and rejuvenated. Sometimes in life that's what we need. We need to have a moment where we go get a refreshing, and in prayer that's where you will receive that the most. We all have those specifics that we pray to God about on a regular basis, but this time I want you to make a list of about five or six key targets that you have *not* prayed about, but which you know that you need to pray over:

Key Prayer Targets: (These prayer targets are what you should be praying over.)

_____

_____

_____

_____

_____

Each day I want you to incorporate your *new* prayer targets listed above in your prayers. Those reasons you did not pray for those listed above no longer exist; they are out the window. Today is a new day! Take some time and really focus on those specifics and see what begins to happen to each target the more that you begin to pray over it. I believe that whatever it is that you have written down has the power to change if you let it. Take a step back after you have prayed about it and let God do the work. Like it says in Philippians 4:6, "Don't worry about anything; instead pray about everything." Don't worry about that financial situation, that unhealthy relationship, your family situation, or that broken friendship, God has it all under control. You just continue to pray your way through. Trust me, God hears your prayers, and he will give you an answer!

A Moment of Honesty:

1. After reading this chapter, are you ready to start the process of forgiving?

    _____

2. If you answered yes, who have you already forgiven them even before talking to them?

    _____

    _____

3. How has your prayer life increased from the person you were in the past to who you are now? What life situation helped shift your prayer life?

    _____

    _____

    _____

    _____

4. Think about that time when it was literally just you and God. What was that experience like? How did it make you feel afterward?

_____

_____

_____

_____

A Note from Tay:

"The woman you are becoming will cost you people, relationships, spaces, and material things. Choose her over everything. Remember that you are one decision away from a totally different life . . . "
Keep being you.

Signed,
Taybrianne

7
Transformation: Mind, Spirit, Environment

"Don't copy the behavior and customs of this world, but let God transform you into a new person by changing the way you think. Then you will learn to know God's will for you, which is good and pleasing and perfect."

— ROMANS 12:2 NEW LIVING TRANSLATION (NLT)

ONE OF THE MAIN REASONS I DESIRED TO WRITE A BOOK about my life, my private pain, and some of my struggles was that I've always told myself that one day, through my transparency, I was going to help other women who went through some of the challenges that I was faced with. This has always been a true passion, yet it didn't fully develop until I was a bit older. So many people would look at me and think that I had it all together. They assumed that because I grew up with a very strong religious background, I had few to no issues and that I was always happy and lived a "perfect life." What those people didn't know was that during much of my adolescence I was depressed and confused because I didn't know who I was. I knew that my name was Taylor, but I didn't know who I was behind all the makeup and clothes. As I shared with you earlier, all I knew for a long time was a life full of cover-ups and hiding. I knew how to pretend like everything was peaches and cream, but when it started becoming noticeable, the hiding eventually had to come to an end. It was in the moment when I became comfortable in my own skin when I discovered my identity and who I was becoming as a woman.

I loved writing even in high school and college. I would always get really good grades on my writing assignments, but I never for one second thought that my love and desire for writing would lead me to writing my very first book. *Ever!* And to be honest, I second-guessed myself quite a bit because I didn't think that I was "intelligent enough" to write a book. I thought that I needed to have a certain language in order to put my thoughts into a book. I tried to talk myself out of it many times, but the more I did that, the more God would continue to give me revelation on what to add in my book. I realized that it's not about being smart enough; it's about your willingness and your obedience to do it. Then God will guide you through the entire process from A to Z and give you exactly what you need to say, using words you never even knew were in your vocabulary.

I believe that transparency makes people more open to share their own pain and hidden secrets—it's when they know that they are not in this alone. My biggest struggle was *identity*. When I see women who have so much potential who battle in this area, especially, it saddens my heart because they either lack support from other women or people in their core who can actually render help; or they simply feel that they are in this by themselves.

When God gave me the name *redefined*, I did not know what "redefined" meant at the time. I just wrote it as I heard it, writing as I began reflecting over my life. It was my twenty-second birthday, and I was sitting on the edge of the bed with tears gushing down my face because I was reminiscing on my journey and all that God had taken me through over the previous couple of years. I instantly went to look up the definition of "redefined," and once it popped up, I began crying even more. The definition of *redefined* according to *Merriam-Webster*: "To reexamine or reevaluate especially with a view to change;" another word was "transform." It was like that definition was created just for my life! Seriously!

I was reevaluated and then given another chance to change my life around for the better. All of those crazy situations had to lead this point, so that the word "redefined" would have so much more meaning for my soul. For that, I will be forever grateful. Every chapter that I talked about in this book, I know so much about it because I've been down each road. From the time of my freedom, I've seen how I've grown spiritually and mentally. I've seen God move me from the back all the way to the front. It was almost like everything was happening so fast and I didn't have time to think; I just had to move as God instructed me to do!

As I was telling one of my mentors about my writing my first book, he asked me a question. "What would you call *this* chapter of your life?" Our life is like a book that includes several chapters. We can close one chapter and begin the next, but it is only from the experiences, the learning moments, and the memories from those previous chapters that travel with us that we can be reminded that there is a brighter future ahead. I can remember having a perplexed look on my face because, first, it caught me off guard and, second, that honestly just never crossed my mind. I didn't have a response—a name to call this chapter of my life—at the time because I had to go back and pray to God what this chapter of my life would be called.

Over the previous two years, I had experienced being at my lowest point, to being able to stand back up, to getting knocked back down. It was almost like things in my life were constantly evolving. People were coming in and leaving. I would be exposed to one thing and move on to the next. During it all, my *identity* became clear. My life was changing. I heard the spirit tell me "*transformation.*"

The Mind

There is nothing more powerful than a change of mind. This is normally the beginning of experiencing total transformation in your life. A transformed mind allows you to see and process what is getting ready to come your way. You can change everything about your outer appearance from your hair style to your clothing, even to your circle of friends, but if you do not change your mindset, you will continue to experience the same cycles repeatedly.

I came to a place in my life where I stopped trying to change people (because you cannot force change on someone; they have to simply want it for themselves) and change my environments, and I started to focus on changing myself. That started in my mind. I started to focus more of my attention on changing my thoughts, my attitudes, and my perception on life, and I began to see that the environment around me changed without me really having to do anything. My prayer was for God to renew my mind. Romans 12:2 lets us know that we are to be *transformed* by the renewing of our mind.

In order for you to experience the total transformation in your life and walk into that season of greatness, it has to begin with your mindset. I could not keep thinking the way that I used to think. I could not keep allowing my life to become consumed by negative thoughts. I could not keep thinking that I can change people. I had to decide, and have my *mind made up*, that I was ready for more. No longer was I going to be comfortable in settings where there was no progress or even spiritual growth. *I needed more.* Simple as that. I became *desperate* for that thing! I was desperate for God to show me his will for my life. I was desperate to live a better lifestyle and be the woman that he created me to be before he even formed me. I was desperate to go from the Girl to the Redefined Woman. I was desperate to not think the same way that I used to and have the same outlook on life when I was just The Girl. I was *desperate*!

How desperate are you? How desperate are you willing to be to experience total transformation, even if it means giving up *everything* just for God to do a shift in your life? Whatever it might be that you truly desire, know that it is achievable by using the power that you have in your mind. Whatever you *think*, you create! David Cuschieri, an author and self-described "heartist," says, "The mind is a powerful force. It can enslave us or empower us. It can plunge us into the depths of misery or take us into the heights of ecstasy. Learn how to use the power wisely." You can create life situations that occur through the power of your mind. If you continue to think that nothing good will ever come your way, that you have to be what this world says you should be, or that you will struggle for the rest of your life, you will see those things begin to manifest. But if you think on these things: *I am the head and not the tail. I am more than enough; I will be the lender and not the borrower; I can do all things through Christ that strengthens me; I am fearfully and wonderfully made; greater is he that is in me than he that is in the world* (Deuteronomy 28:13, Deuteronomy 15:6, Philippians 4:13, Psalms 139:14, and 1 John 4:4), you'll start to believe it. But it all starts in the mind.

Some of you find yourself tossing and turning at night; you can't sleep because you're constantly thinking. You're consistently thinking about the "what ifs"—all the bad that could happen—and thinking about all that is out of your control. That was a big issue for me. The enemy would paint these pictures in my mind, especially at night, of all the bad that possibly could happen, and for a moment I started to believe it because I would do it so often.

One picture that the enemy would frequently paint in my mind was death. I would always see pictures of caskets and get so afraid that I had to start pleading the blood of Jesus over my thoughts. Satan's greatest attack came at night when my mind would just begin to race, thinking about any and everything. I had the power to change that situation through my prayer. Even in this moment, I release over your life that you will experience peace at night! You will be able to experience rest without your thoughts and certain images keeping you up at night.

You have the power to change your situation the moment that you change your way of thinking. The past is only supposed to be a memory that should have no power over you unless you choose to focus all your attention there. Transformation happens when you *stop living in your head*!

The Spirit

I learned to use my mind to piece together the lessons from my past mistakes. Every day I was working on being better; making my life better, including things around me. It meant living a happier life. As a result, I began to develop a different type of spirit. When I say spirit in this context, I mean *attitude. Life is 10 percent what happens to you and 90 percent how you react to it.* So much of what I see today is that women feel obligated to react or respond to *everything*! How do I know? Because that was me! Straight up, I always felt the need to respond to *everything* or felt like I just had to get in the last word. That's an area of my life which I am consistently working on improving. Don't get me wrong, there are certain things and situations that might require you to speak up or react to, especially if it is life or death. If you *know* that your response and your reaction are not going to change the current situation, then it's best that you *leave it alone*! We as women are in charge of our attitude. *We* are in charge of our behavior and emotions and how we choose to act out during certain situations.

We are emotional by nature, so it's likely for us to respond or react first and then think about it later after the fact. As a kid, my attitude was awful! I saw how it started to impact my adulthood, so I knew it needed to be dealt with.

The problem with most of us is that we struggle with controlling and containing our attitude. We are emotional by nature, so it's likely for us to respond or react first and then think about it later after the fact. As a kid, my attitude was awful! I saw how it started to impact my adulthood, so I knew it needed to be dealt with. And it's OK to admit your issues. Trust me! I had to confront my issue face to face and figure out ways to deal with that problem.

Some of us can become very defensive, or our first instinct is to put up this guard to protect ourselves and retaliate anytime someone tells us the truth about who we are. Perhaps something may even be said to us that we know we need to hear but we don't want to accept what is said because deep down inside we don't like the truth. Don't feel like you are always being attacked or feel like you always have to respond. Sometimes hearing the truth about your attitude or about who you are when it's coming from the right person is meant to help develop you into a more mature woman, and it begins with a self-reflection of your attitude. Anybody who knows me can tell you that I am extremely sensitive. I wear my emotions on my sleeve. Because I am sensitive, I would always feel like I was being attacked or people were saying things about me that I knew were true, but my emotions led me to believe that these were said to deliberately hurt me. The more I matured and heard the same statements, but from different people who meant me no harm, it really made me check myself and evaluate my attitude. Over time, I matured spiritually, which became a huge help for improving my attitude toward life, my attitude toward me, and my attitude toward others. Eventually, I realized that those small adjustments, such as not always lashing back but learning how to just listen, made a huge difference in my life. Transformation was not just about me altering my mind or the posture of my heart, but it was about changing who I was on the outside.

What do others see when they see you? When I experienced transformation in my attitude and lifestyle, it became evident to those who were around me quite frequently, especially to my close friends. I let go of certain environments such as the club scene and hanging out late at certain spots that I knew would not be beneficial to my growth. I spent more time alone, and in that period, I got to know more about myself. I found out who Taylor really was. I began working on certain areas of my life that needed to be strengthened. My relationship with God truly started to grow deeper. Deeper than ever before. I completely stopped drinking. For almost three years, that was my biggest stronghold, and I knew that deliverance would only come if I removed it completely from my life. I had to admit it to myself that it was a huge struggle. As a result, my walk towards a healthier lifestyle became a bit easier. There was evidence of personal growth because I was happier, and I would always find myself encouraging and motivating others. I became unashamed to tell my story to whomever needed to hear it. I would pray for anybody who needed it. My walk with Christ was no longer an option but it became my priority! *Unapologetic*!

You never know who is watching you. People are constantly paying attention to how you carry yourself, how you respond, and what type of spirit you are carrying. I ask God now more than ever to give me the ability to discern a spirit. Help me to look past the outer and see a person for who they are based on their behavior and their motives. Trust a person for who they are beyond what you see on the outside. How do they think? How do they speak? What is the ultimate reason behind why they do what they do? Even with yourself. What are your motives? How do others perceive you? You will always be remembered for the first impression you leave with others. First impressions are *everything*. Take some time and really do an evaluation of your attitude. If there is something that needs to be fixed, handle it! You'd be surprised at what you might discover.

The Environment

I knew there was *more* that God wanted from me, and there was more that I wanted from him, but it could not happen where I was. When God called Abraham while he was with his family in his hometown, he specifically gave him instructions to leave his country, his family, and his father's home; to leave *everything* behind and *go* to this land that he wanted to show him (Genesis 12). Abraham had no idea where he was going; he did not ask questions, nor did he know what was going to be there when he got to the land. All he knew was that it was time for him to *go*. He knew that his blessing was not going to happen where he was. He knew that he wouldn't have the level of faith that he did had he not been obedient. He understood that there was obviously more that God wanted to use him for, so he took that leap of faith, trusted God, and he went! Obedience.

My environment was the hardest part of my period of transformation. The mind and the spirit were a bit easier, but when it came to my needing to detach myself from certain places or even people, I was apprehensive. I looked at the outcome as one in which I would be alone, instead of what actually awaited me, which was being rewarded with what was better. I knew that it was time for a better lifestyle; I knew that it was time for me to *go*. I knew that I was outgrowing that specific place, but I just didn't know exactly where to begin. I loved being around the people that I was around with and hanging out with them every weekend. But God wouldn't let me stay there.

During my undergraduate years, I was working at a clothing store called H&M. Many of you no doubt are familiar with it. My season in retail was *definitely* coming to an end, however, because I had no desire whatsoever to continue working. It was so draining, and I was ready for something new. I hated coming to work. It was just paying the little bills that I had at the time, which is why I stayed there as long as I did. I never had a weekend to myself because I was always at work until late.

One day I received a phone call right before my early morning shift began—I remember being at the register ten minutes before the store opened when my phone rang. I was auditing my drawer, but as soon as I got the call, totally unexpected, I *ran* to the bathroom. (I almost lost my job because I was on the clock, on the phone, hiding in the bathroom.) I had gotten a call from a prospective employer calling me with a job offer . . . and it was for a *better* job. It would involve a new environment, new experiences, new people, but the same *God!* It was a little scary at the moment because I just couldn't believe that it all happened so fast. *Go! Leave!* is what I kept hearing.

Prior to that, I had applied for many different jobs elsewhere, gone to many interviews, and gotten rejected each time. My aggressive pursuit of employment elsewhere had reached the point where I was being told to quit calling and following up, that they had decided to pursue other candidates. I have never received so much rejection in my life. It had gotten so bad that I was told by one prospective employer that I should consider applying somewhere else because I wasn't qualified enough. I didn't understand why it was happening, because every other job I'd ever interviewed for I had gotten—in most cases on the spot. Once again, I felt rejected. But God truly had other plans.

I couldn't keep quiet, so I immediately called my mom and my brother and told them the news that I had just received. I remember them telling me that my life was going to change *forever* and that I would no longer be able to bring my old habits and old ways into this new place. *Transformation.*

Day 1 in this new environment was the next Monday. I was so excited after accepting the job, yet I was nervous. I cried tears of joy, astonished because I could not believe what had just happened. Instantly, I felt that this new place was going to help me do a complete turnaround. The more that I was devoted to this environment, the more I began to see small changes in my lifestyle. I had a different outlook on life. My attitude changed. I saw what greatness looked like. I saw the behind the scenes of entrepreneurs. I saw how to be a leader and not just any leader but an *effective* leader. Who knew that God would trust me enough to be a personal assistant to such an amazing woman, Dr. Stephaine Walker. Whatever she needed me to do, I was more than willing to do it. At the time, she was still practicing medicine, so I would always help her stay organized with her schedule, help her put together events, attend meetings with her, and I even had the opportunity to do some traveling. I was amazed at what I would see on a regular basis.

I saw hard work, commitment, dedication, and sleepless nights, and I definitely saw *favor* not only over her life but over her husband's life as well. The more they would do for other people out of the kindness of their heart, the more God would continue to bless them. Most importantly, I noticed that my relationship with God began to grow deeper because of whom I was connected to. It became *authentic*. It was a fire that had just been burned down on the inside of me like never before to really pursue God. All it takes is that *one* connection, that one phone call, that one person who will completely change your life forever. All God needs to do is pick you up from where you are and put you around the right people, in the right environment, at the right time, to experience total transformation.

The journey in this space was all about being developed, being stretched, being challenged, and being motivated. It's crazy how God works. You pray for exposure to more experiences, or you pray for a new environment, and he gives you that. But he gives it to you in a way where it might make you uncomfortable. It could mean you're having to use skill sets that you never knew existed. It might mean to speak in front of people you never expected to be in the same room with. You might experience constructive criticism, and it might humble you. In the end, though, you can look back at it and understand that it was necessary. You understand that it *had* to happen.

Your environment is all about your exposure. It's all about what you see on a regular basis or the type of people with whom you are connected. I was blessed to be connected with the Walker family!

I don't think God could have connected me with any couple better than the two people that he brought into my life. He brought them into my life just when I felt like completely giving up. They came when I felt like God had given up on me. They have helped me in so many ways; if I tried to begin to talk about it all, I'd probably need a few more chapters to do so. I never had the business woman/entrepreneur mindset prior to meeting Dr. Steph and Bishop Walker. I always knew that I wanted to be successful, but I never thought it would come down to me wanting to have something to call my own, such as this book.

I saw how hard they worked day in and day out. A lot of sleep had been sacrificed, from business meetings to board meetings, to conference calls, to travel almost every other week, to ministry, I mean the whole nine yards and they *still* made sure that they got the job done. *Effectively!* The most important lesson that I learned was that you work hard now and invest every chance that you get so that you can enjoy life in the future. One thing Dr. Steph would always tell me is, "You do what you have to do when you have to do it, so that you can do what you want to do when you want to do it."

Although I was her personal assistant, she never made me feel like that. She made me feel like I was a part of their family. There is such level of respect that I have for this woman. She always pushed me to be *above* average. To set goals. To never quit. Most importantly, to have a vision! (*Without a vision, the people perish.*) The idea is to work hard *now*, while I have the chance, while I'm still young, so that in the end, it will certainly pay off. She told me it's good to have tunnel vision, but it's even better to have a landscape view.

Her husband, Bishop Joseph W. Walker III, taught me the importance of maintaining my relationship with God. He was there for me as a spiritual guide. There had been many moments where I felt stuck and had no clue where my life was headed or even why God allowed it to be *me*, and there's one thing that he said to me that I will never forget! Sitting there in his office, he looked me in the eye as tears began to roll down the side of my face, and he said to me, "You are *chosen*." The same word that was spoken over me as a young girl meant more to me *now* than ever. This time I really felt that! *I believed it*! I understood it! It clicked! He told me that God was not just exposing me to all that I had seen for the fun of it; he was giving me a preview of what was going to be mine! ("Everywhere the soles of your feet touch shall be *yours*.")

I also learned the importance of *family*. The *core*! No matter how hard the two had been working, or how long of a day they had put in, they always made sure that family was No. 1 on their list. From family vacations to something simple as taking their little princess Jovanni Willow Walker (that's my baby) to get ice cream as a family after school, they did it! They've shown me that no matter how busy life gets, with God being first, family is more important! To sum that up, life is all about *balance*!

So, having said all of that, I have a few questions that I want you to answer:

1. What are two things in your life currently that you are *desperate* to change about who you are?

_____

_____

2. When others see you, how would they perceive you? What type of impression do you believe that you leave based on your behavior?

_____

_____

_____

3. What kind of environment are you exposed to on a daily basis? Has there been a continual pull or a constant push?

_____

_____

_____

Your environment is all about what you are being exposed to. A changed mindset and behavior will be the stepping stones that will lead you there. When God gives you instructions to leave a certain thing or place, you must be *obedient* and do it! *Go!* You don't know what he is trying to do for you or where he might be trying to take you to bless you. This is not the season for you to ask questions, to be contemplating, or to be fearful. When you hear the word *go*, you know that it is time!

Since my committing to my obedience and acting on my willingness to go ahead and leave some stuff behind, God began doing things that blew my mind. My exposure pushed me even more to want to be transformed. It pushed me to think at a higher level, to have a plan and execute, to be motivated from the hard work that I have seen. It pushed me to be innovative and do something that nobody in my generation has ever done. With the support of the right people in your corner and with the right mindset, attitude, and environment, what's stopping you now from being creative? You can research, read books, read articles, watch videos on how to be successful or how to be a millionaire all day long, but all it takes is for you to *see* one good time how it's done and have a clear visual of the possibility that is made available to you, and then to achieve it! But remember . . . greatness lies within you; you just have to begin to birth it *out* of you!

A Note from Tay:

"We will never know what that moment of giving birth is like until it's our time to begin pushing . . . "

Signed,
Taybrianne

8
The P.U.S.H. (Proceed Until Shifting Happens)

"Whatever is good and perfect is a gift coming down to us from God our father, who created all the lights in the heavens. He never changes or casts a shifting shadow."

— JAMES 1:17 NEW LIVING TRANSLATION (NLT)

The Position

When we think about birth or the delivery of a baby, it *normally* is affiliated with pain. Some women who have given birth tend to associate birth with the amount of pain they've had to endure. Most don't even consider having a natural birth because they don't want to experience the unanesthetized labor pains. As a result, they seek the necessary medication. Typically, that is called an epidural. An epidural is known to be the most effective method for pain relief during labor.

During the labor process, depending on which stage of labor the mother might be in, different positions assist in the progress of the labor. For example, the upright position encourages the baby to descend into the birth canal. This position gives more room to the fetus for rotation and descent. This position helps to make the pushing process a little less challenging. If the mother is not in the proper position or the fetus does not seem to adjust well to the positioning of the mother's body during the process, this might cause a delay in the pushing. Such an extended labor period is accompanied by an increase in the level of pain, and it can increase the risk of something happening to the *gift*.

Some of you are carrying a special seed inside of you that is ready to be delivered. The contractions have begun, you feel the kicks, you feel the pain, and the urge is to get it out of you. There's no more delay in the process because you've been carrying that seed for too long. There is a certain posture that you must be in, for you to give birth to your special gift. To be ready, you must position yourself to be able to *push!* To be in the right position, you need to position your mind, your attitude, your focus, and your *life* to be in alignment with the will of God. God is the giver of gifts! So, he gives you what he knows you need for that greatness to come all the way out of you.

There is a certain posture that you must be in, for you to give birth to your special gift. To be ready, you must position yourself to be able to PUSH!

Understand that you do not become good by trying to just be good; you become good by finding that goodness that is already within you and allowing that goodness to be *birthed*. (I call this "positioning your focus.") I discussed in the last chapter about changing your mind, but you position it by thinking positive. Don't allow any negativity, doubt, worry, or fear to enter your mind; avoid coming up with excuses that will try to prevent you from going through with your delivery process.

The positioning of your attitude determines your altitude. A strong, positive, and resilient attitude will help you reach higher levels in life. The positioning of your mind, your attitude, and your focus all work together to position your life to be in direct alignment with God.

Some of you were born specifically for greatness. Since you were a little girl, you probably had very unique gifts, talents, skills, etc. that you were very good at, yet you never really had anybody in your corner to help you push it/them all the way out of you except for maybe that one person. You know who that one person is—that one person who has always been there since the beginning. That person whose voice you would always hear in the back of your head whenever you found yourself in trouble. You might hear them say, "Girl, you being real crazy right now . . . " or that voice that reminds you, "Sis, you don't deserve to be treated like that. Leave his butt alone." Or perhaps it's that one person who was the first person with whom you shared your vision or your dream, and they believed in it more than you did. That person is the one who is going to help you through your birthing process. Like the mother, she had all these voices speaking to her, encouraging her, helping her through the pushing process; yet, how did she know that all who were in the room speaking really wanted her to have a successful delivery?

The Push

How did the mother know that everyone who was motivating and encouraging her were truthful about it? She assumed everybody was on her side, right? Better yet . . . how did she know for certain that everybody in the delivery room was actually expecting for that gift that the mother was carrying for months would someday be a world changer? Typically, you think of these people to be just like family or close friends, and you would not for one second question the sincerity in their support. "Come on, you can do this!" "*Breathe!*" "*Push!*" "It's almost *out!*"

Does every person in your circle really want to see you succeed? Are they supportive from the heart, or do they feel forced to support because "we're friends"? Can they even handle the level of greatness that you are carrying? I learned the hard way that not everybody will support you; not everybody will believe in you. There will be only a handful of people who want to see you win; you will lose friends simply because God has elevated you. There are ideas, visions, plans, and even goals that I wish I had never shared with certain individuals. There are some people I wish I had never been open with because later I found out that you must be careful about whom you share information with and allow to speak over your life. You must use discernment when sharing visions from God with other people. Sometimes, their own prayer might be that your vision will fail or be ineffective and that it won't manifest simply because of the jealousy and envy they have within their hearts. Be careful of whom you allow into your "delivery room."

Some people will have to stay in the waiting room because their eyes are not mature enough to see what God is getting ready to birth out of you! Get around some people who are *with* you! Get around some people who *want* to see you *win*! Get around some people who are authentically there with you through the entire birthing process, no matter how long it takes!

For you to experience greatness, you will have to push. A due date is given because there is a certain time frame of expectancy for the seed to be carried inside. Eventually that seed is going to be exposed to the world. The same applies to you. God has given you a due date for the moment in which you will deliver. You know what that gift is because you have been given a glimpse of what it is. Just like an ultrasound, you are given a small visual of what your seed looks like. You can't see everything just yet, but you get a small visual of the basic structures. You've already been given a glimpse of what your seed is going to look like. When will you be ready to push it out of you?

Take a moment and think about that gift that you know God has placed inside of you:

1. What is that gift inside of you that just will not sleep; no matter how many times you try and get comfortable, it always seems to keep you up at night?

_____

2. How are you going to position yourself to be prepared for the delivery of your gift?

_____

_____

3. Ask yourself this: Am I ready for the birthing process, no matter if it's short and sweet or long and painful?

_____

Small Beginnings

One of my new favorite scriptures is Zechariah 4:10: "Do *not* despise that day of small beginnings, for the Lord rejoices to see the work begin." It's not when you start that matters; all that matters is that you *start*. Just because you haven't "made it to the top yet" does not mean that what you are doing now doesn't matter. It's the simplest things, those "small beginnings," that help get you to the next level in life. Therefore, you can't take those simple moments for granted because they are imperative. Carol O'Connor, author of the book *Secrets of Great Leaders*, shared a quote by American statesman Colin Powell, an American statesman, that really sparked my attention: "If you are going to achieve excellence in big things, you develop the habit in small matters. Excellence is not an exception, it is a prevailing attitude."[4] What you do with the little you have will reflect what you do when God blesses you with more. Don't overlook the small investments.

The only thing that gets in the way of your being great is *you*. The only person standing in the way of your getting to that Redefining Moment is *you*. The small investments that you are making now and the small tasks that you are completing now, the resources that you are using now, will impact your destiny. We as women are always viewed as being weak or less powerful and that we can't do anything without the "help of a man," but the issue is that we have to stop looking for men to always do things for us that we can do for ourselves. You get you a "boo," or you're in a relationship, and now you feel like because you have this man in your life, you should always look to him to do everything for you. So then when you find yourself in a crisis situation and he's nowhere to be found, you're going insane and don't know what to do. You've become so dependent on this one person to do absolutely *Everything* for you.

C'mon, sis. There's too much greatness inside of you to not have some level of independence. Learn how to make things happen for yourself even if nobody around you is supportive of that vision. Learn how to use what you have right in front of you right *now* to start unfolding the totality of greatness. Like the woman who is giving birth, although she has the physicians, the nurses, and family there as support, she is the only one who can do the pushing. In order to give birth to the gift, the vision, the idea, the innovation, the greatness that is being carried, *you* have to push! So, position yourself because it's time.

Check the people who you have in the delivery room with you because you will need the right eyes around you to see what is getting ready to come out. The birthing process is but for a moment. Later, that excruciating pain will be over, and it will be so worth it. I encourage you today, to begin to push out that gift, push out that dream, and push out those ideas and that vision. Push out that greatness inside. Even if you are the only one in the room, with no support, honey, you'd better push until it is all the way out! . . . C'mon, you got it! *Push*!!!!!

A Moment of Honesty:

1. Who are the three people in your life right now who have been the most influential and supportive when it comes to the birthing process of your gift?

_____

_____

_____

2. Would you agree that your posture right now to give birth to your gift is The Upright Position? If you disagreed, what is preventing you from being in the proper position?

_____

A Note from Tay:

This year is going to be the year that things will begin to manifest in your own life. You have prayed, you've cried, you've fasted, you've written everything out, now it's time to sit back and watch how everything that you have been believing God for is going to happen! . . . Real fast at that . . . so get ready!

Keep believing.

Signed,
Taybrianne

9
The Greater *You*

*"For I can do everything through Christ
who gives me strength."*

— PHILIPPIANS 4:13 NEW LIVING TRANSLATION (NLT)

YOU HOLD THE MASTER KEY THAT UNLOCKS THE DOOR TO greatness. Greatness is manifested not by being fake, but it emerges when you practice authenticity. Authenticity means being totally and completely yourself at any given time. It's not trying to make the world believe that you are this person who claims to be skilled in organization, time management, and communication, when you really know you have a hard time staying organized, are always the last one to show up for functions, and you don't know how to talk to people because you say whatever comes to mind. Acknowledging that you need to be strengthened in certain areas is a sign of maturity and humility, it means that you are willing to do what it takes to experience greatness.

It's sad to see how this world has distorted the true meaning of authenticity. Nothing that we do or see anymore is authentic. We have been shown by some people that in order to "make it" in this world, you have to be phony, conniving, and selfish. Take reality TV, for example. Like the reality series *Love and Hip-Hop*. This media franchise's first episode aired on March 6, 2011. It is one of a variety of television series that are broadcast on VH1. As one of the highest-rated "unscripted" franchises in cable television history, this series is known for its sprawling cast with more than two hundred members from the East Coast, West Coast, and Southern hip-hop.

This show documents the personal and professional lives of several different hip-hop and R&B musicians, including producers, managers, and performers. There has been much controversy since the launch of the show as critics have been led to believe that much of the narrative is fabricated. In my view, it is a reality TV program that is demoralizing not only toward women, but it has a way of downplaying one's manhood. It's rare that you will ever receive an uplifting and empowering message from watching the show. Shows such as these have contributed to brainwashing and deceiving of a rising generation into believing that the achievement of success and/or wealth requires us to portray ourselves to the world as something that we are not. We are assembling a generation that believes being foolish in front of a camera is what's going to get you recognition.

We see women spending thousands of dollars to add to or take away from what God originally created and then being depicted on social media as "body goals." Young girls are being misled to believe that fake everything is the new "IT." All we hear in the lyrics of this new genre of music from rising young rappers are drugs, sex, money, and violence as we watch them take home awards, live in luxury homes, and drive around in the most expensive cars. We have young men who don't even want to go to school anymore and pursue a higher education. They don't have the drive or the passion to become the next doctor or lawyer because they see how quick money can be made, so what's the use of them even working hard? They have no desire to be a faithful man or to one day be a husband because the word *commitment* scares them!

No one seems to be teaching our young women how to be a lady, how to act like a lady, how to speak and dress like a young woman with class and dignity instead of only wanting a man for his money. Because he claims he loves you and "says" you're the only one, you feel obligated to give it up. How does someone you barely know even deserve your special treasure? Is that really the authentic you? This generation will continue to allow the entertainment, music, and reality TV industries to greatly influence their decisions or behavior as long as there is silence concerning this matter.

How is it that people are being inspired by foolishness and ignorance? Of course, some people work hard for what they want, but what kind of motivation do we have that is actually pushing us to be ourselves, beyond our trying to a live a life just for an audience? We must get back to being *authentic*. And it can start with *you*!

You don't have to be in front of a camera pretending to be something that you are not just to survive and say you've done something. There is more that will be extended to you when you represent the real you. We have to rise up, take a stand, and come together as women and show others what it really means to be real! The only way that we will conquer the odds against us is by being the best version of ourselves. Go back to finding out who and what you truly are. That's spending some time *alone*! That's the only way you will be able to experience greatness for yourself!

Companions and *Not* Competitors

I once heard my pastor teach a message during one Bible study that was an absolute blessing to my life. He talked about how God has created us to be companions—meaning that we are all to work together for one greater purpose, which is to fulfill the works of the kingdom of God. He broke it down ever further and said that when we compare ourselves to the next person, we start to compete. What we've then done is turned what they have and what we have and make it a competition. We must prove to them that although you might be good, I can be better. It's almost tit for tat.

When we start to compete, we ultimately disrupt the original plan that God has for our lives, which is to work together so that we can all experience greatness. If you have not learned one thing throughout the course of this book, I want you to know this: There is power when *we*, especially as women, come together! That is a huge statement. We have the power to change this world as women working together! We have the power to turn this world upside down! There is so much respect that comes from the right kinds of people when they see women doing things that have been classified as "a man's job," especially when we do it together.

I read Bishop T. D. Jakes's book *Soar*, and let me just tell you that if you have the mindset of an entrepreneur, or you want to develop that mindset, that book will absolutely be a blessing to your life. I encourage you to read it. In the book, Bishop Jakes talks about how women have more of an advantage then men in most instances. He cited statistics of how African-American women control 14 percent of the major companies across the United States, which is roughly about 1.3 million businesses. Going even deeper, he shared how the number of businesses owned by African-American women had grown 332 percent since 1997, making black women the *fastest*-growing group of entrepreneurs in the United States! That blew my mind, OK!?

Women are taking over in these different industries because of the creativity and the innovation they have. Believe it or not, we women bring a lot to the table, but we have to show these different industries why women deserve a seat. The moral of the story is, we got it going on, and although these statistics were geared toward black women, know that as women, regardless of ethnicity, we rock, period! Please ma'am, know that it is OK to support or congratulate the success level of the next woman. It is OK every now and again to send someone a random text message and say, *"I'm proud of you."*

There is absolutely no reason for us to compete with one another because we all can make it, living lavish lifestyles and having nice things. Imagine it! Imagine being your own boss of your own company or organization, clothing store or beauty salon, having your own dance studio or starting your own daycare center. *You can do it!* You need the support of other like-minded women who have been where you are trying to go, or such women who are currently in route. Be supportive and remain *humble*! God honors humility. We are blessed when we learn how to remain humble and not prideful. Stop always making it about yourself and pretentiously thinking that you have to go above and beyond just to be noticed. People notice humility and they tend to support you more when you are not always making it about yourself. When you focus on the bigger picture, which means trying to positively impact the lives of others, it gives others a reason to want to offer support. The more God blesses you, the lower you need to be. *Stay low!*

Get yourself a good mentor—someone who is a good role model for what you are trying to become in life. Your mentor should be someone to look up to and learn from, but you should never try to be exactly like her or him. I shared with you earlier about my mentor. She is fantastic, and I tell her all the time how much I have learned just by watching how she works, how she operates, and how she carries herself as a woman. This lady is *no joke* and she makes things happen, which is what I love about her the most. Even with making things happen, she is the sweetest, most loving, caring, and giving person I have ever known. She has much wisdom to offer, and her intelligence is truly off the charts. Every time I have come to her for advice or wisdom about life's circumstances, she has *always* steered me in the right direction. Primarily, it's because she has been in my shoes, so she knows exactly what she is talking about. Whoever that person is for you, it must be someone who can give you the best possible advice toward life's situations. They should never steer you in the wrong direction, but they should always be there to make sure that you become the best possible version of yourself. Take notes of the steps and the tools that have helped them get to where they are in their life. Don't live your life trying to copy someone else's life!

Your Life . . . His Way

Remember that God has a plan and a purpose for your life. In that plan he has created something so great and powerful that separates you from those around you. God will never create a thing and then try to figure out how he is going to use it or what he is going to do with it. He has already factored that in prior to creating something. When God created man, he formed him from the dust of the ground, breathed the breath of life into the man's nostrils, and *then* he became a living person. He then created the Garden of Eden and placed man in the garden to watch over it and tend it. God did not create Adam only to then try and decide what he was going to do with this human being to whom he had just given life; he had a purpose already designed for him.

The same goes for you. God knew everything about you and had an outline of your life even before he created you. (Read Jeremiah 1:5. This scripture blesses me *every time*. I promise it will do the same for you!) You might think that because you are not where you want to be or think you should be in life at this moment, that it means you will be stuck where you are forever. It is only temporary! It is only a season that you must go through so that you understand what it's like to experience the fullness of greatness. The pain that the mother felt during the delivery process was only temporary. For her to push the gift out, she had to be willing to endure the temporary moment of pain.

The good thing about being on the road to greatness is that you never stay in one place forever. Elevation is always made available to you, but only if you are willing and obedient to God's instruction. Every overachiever or world changer has a story. Think about Oprah Winfrey. A little girl from Mississippi, born out of wedlock, lived in the ghetto as a child, suffered from abuse and rape by a cousin, uncle, and family friend. She was fired from her very first television job as an anchor in Baltimore, where she was faced with sexism and harassment. Even through the midst of all of that, she is known *today* as one of the world's most successful women, as well as one of its wealthiest. Oprah could have easily given up after being fired; she could have easily allowed the trauma she experienced in her childhood to eat her up every single day; but she *knew* that her plan was for a greater purpose than what she'd seen or experienced. The plan for her life was greater than her first rejection, and I'm sure it was greater than her own desires. The more work that you put in, the more you will experience elevation; the more you'll begin to see the light at the end of the tunnel.

It's our life . . . but it's God's way! Stop trying to plan everything out about your life from A to Z because at any given moment that whole agenda can be changed. (I had to learn that the hard way. I am a huge planner! I plan everything, and I tried to plan out how my life was going to play out from start to finish . . . until God had to *force* me to stop relying on myself and to rely more on him.) Stop looking at your situation and thinking the worse, believing that where you are right now *is* your final destination. Maybe he hasn't shown your where he is getting ready to take you yet or what he wants to give to you, because if he does it prematurely, it might scare you, you might be intimidated, you might run from it and never come back. It could be that God is trying to develop you, mature you, build you, and stretch your faith so that when the time is right he will know that you are ready. You just have to understand that he is *God!* There is nothing too hard for him, and he can use anybody that he chooses. His word says that he is *able* (meaning he has the power) to do *exceedingly, abundantly, above all* that we can ask or think. So, what you imagine for yourself or what you have believed God for is simple compared to what he envisions for you. He can do more than that! What he has for you is going to be something greater than what you have imagined. Just wait on it!

My desire for you is that you will not allow your circumstances or your pain to hinder you from experiencing the manifestation of greatness that is getting ready to happen in your life. You have to be a witness of how God still allowed you to walk into greatness even in the midst of your broken-ness. As I have spoken before, greatness is already in you; it's there, and once you allow God to not just heal you, but to make you *whole*, you will really be able to see it for yourself . . . just watch!

"*Wholeness does not mean perfection: It means embracing brokenness as an integral part of life.*" *(Parker Palmer)*

A Moment of Honesty:

1. On a scale of 1 to 10, with 10 being the highest, how suc-cessful have you been in preparation for the road toward greatness?

_____

2. How many times have you found yourself in competi-tion with another person or comparing yourself to her/his qualities without even realizing it? How did that make you feel? *Be honest!*

_____

_____

A Note from Tay:

"Stepping onto a brand-new path is difficult, but not more difficult than remaining in a situation, which is not nurturing to the whole woman."

— MAYA ANGELOU

10
A Whole New *You*

"And he said to her, 'Daughter, your faith has made you well. Go in peace. Your suffering is over.'"
— MARK 5:34 NEW LIVING TRANSLATION (NLT)

Whole
/hol/
adjective
2. in an unbroken or undamaged state; in one piece.

IN *ONE* PIECE . . . NO LONGER A MILLION PIECES SHATTERED IN A million different places. Just *one*! God is getting ready to put you back together again, but this time as one. You are no longer broken or damaged. This is the season when you will be put back together from the inside out. Do you believe that? Being made whole on the outside is one thing, but when God makes you whole spiritually (on the inside) it's a whole different experience. When God makes you whole spiritually, your perspective and attitude toward life will change. Everything around you begins to change.

You no longer try to do things your own way. Your connection is more real than it has ever been before; Jesus becomes your priority and not an option!

You notice that you have more love within your heart. You make communicating with God a lifestyle and not just on special occasions. You can hear him speak to you more; you are more in tune with him; you are able to discern; you listen to his voice before making critical decisions; and you are constantly reminding yourself of what his word says any time you feel like you are about to give up. Each day you are finding new ways to strive to be a better woman, and that's by allowing the Spirit of God to lead you in every direction that you need to go. You no longer try to do things your own way. Your connection is more real than it has ever been before; Jesus becomes your priority and not an option!

Think about the woman with the issue of blood. I'm sure you have heard about her. If not, let me introduce you to her. This woman had been struggling for twelve long years with a bleeding condition that wouldn't stop. She had gone to many physicians to receive help for her condition, but nothing worked. In fact, her condition got worse. She spent everything that she had on trying to receive help from people, only for them to tell her there was nothing left for them to do. She knew that she needed another kind of healing from someone other than the people who could do nothing for her. She needed spiritual healing! She got it in her mind that if she could just touch a portion of Jesus's robe, she would be healed. She was willing to do whatever it took for her to get to the one who could heal her from her terrible and excruciating condition.

Between what she spoke out of her mouth and the touch of the robe, the healing power of Jesus that transferred to this woman had been activated because immediately this woman was healed. That condition that was causing her pain, causing her to toss and turn at night, causing her to seek out others to heal her, causing her to be on her face crying every night—a condition that she had been living with for years—had just been removed. All because of what she believed and declared out of her mouth.

Out of all the people who were standing in that crowd, Jesus felt this woman's touch. He felt her pain. He felt her need of spiritual wholeness. He felt the desperation that she had to be healed completely from everything that she ever done in her past. She hid nothing back from him because she needed something deeper than just a healing. Jesus became her *priority*! She fell at his feet, and she was honest with him about everything that was going on in her life. Where man had failed her, *Christ* succeeded. It wasn't because of who she was, the extent of her condition, or the longevity of her bleeding, or the garment that she touched, but it was her *faith*! Her faith caused the power of God to perform a miracle. Her faith caused her to receive not just a healing but *wholeness*! "And he said to her daughter your *faith* has made you whole." (Mark 5:34)

How much *faith* do you have to believe that you can and *will* be made whole? That you are already whole before it even happens? How honest are you willing to be with Jesus even though he already knows it all? Like the woman, for her faith to have made her whole, she had to believe that it was already done. How did she believe? She spoke it before it even happened. "Speak to those things that be *not* as though they already are." Today you *will* be whole. Your *faith* is what is going to bring about spiritual wholeness in your life.

As *The Broken Girl*, I never once imagined that I would be half the woman that I am today. It never clicked to me back then that I have the power to someday grow up and be a world changer. I was content with where I was because that was comfortable enough for me. I really wasn't too excited about the outcome of my future because I was so focused on the troubles and challenges of life in my present.

During that time, I was in a constant battle with my identity, so I had absolutely no clue about who I was. It took my going through experiences, being faced with adversity, getting knocked down to my lowest point, to realize that I didn't have to be this way forever. This is only a small snippet to my testimony. As the days and months went by, it clicked that someday I would have a story to tell that would inspire women that although you've experienced brokenness, you can be made *whole* again. And so, I *believed* it! I spoke it until I started to see it become reality!

When God breaks us, he does it with such purpose to put us back together, this time better than before. Tasha Cobbs, a phenomenal gospel singer, said it best in her song "Gracefully Broken": "God will break you to position you, break you to promote you, break you to put you in your right place, but when he breaks you he doesn't hurt you; when he breaks you he doesn't destroy you, he does it with *grace!*" *Grace is God's power.* It is what sustained you when the enemy tried everything in his power to destroy you and take you out. Grace is that *gift* that we don't even deserve. None of us! God was so gracious about the way that he broke you. He meant no harm by it. He had it all planned out about how he was going to do it. He knew that you wouldn't like the way that it felt, but he was certain that it was necessary so that you could be made *whole!* Like the woman with the issue of blood—her pain was *necessary* because it helped to activate her faith in God to where she believed that it was already done even before it happened! She wouldn't have a story that we still hear about even today had she not gone through her season of pain.

You've Made It!

Smile because your best days are ahead of you! Smile because you have way too much to be grateful and thankful for. Don't be afraid to share your testimony with those around you. There are people in this world who need to hear your story. They need to hear how you made it out of that abusive relationship; they need to hear how you were once lost but now you are found, they need to know how soul ties kept you bound for years. *But God*! Someone needs to hear how you struggled with self-love, self-respect, and knowing who you are, but now you are at a place where you love yourself now more than ever for whom God has created you to be.

Don't be ashamed to let others know that there is no perfect family, and we all might suffer from some form of dysfunction, but God is a restorer and he can mend any broken family and make them one again. Let the world know that the only attention that you need is that from God, because that's all that matters. He has already validated you and you've been stamped by his approval. Be the representation of what authenticity looks like. Show this generation what an authentic relationship with God is like. And if you have to be the only one doing it, *do it*!

Let your faith take you places that you can't see with your eyes right now. Let your belief get you a seat at the table with people that you never once imagined you'd be around. Let God do the work; in the meantime, you stay planted, stay committed, stay humble, stay faithful, and, most importantly, stay obedient. Remain true to yourself and don't be shaken by anybody.

Ladies, stand your ground! Stand up for who you are as a new woman. This brand-new season that you are getting ready to embark on is about the change in your life *forever*! People are going to look at you and notice that you are not the same girl that you used to be. They are going to look at you and see you as a brand-new woman.

A Note from Tay:

"Difficult roads often lead to beautiful destinations. . . . Wow! . . . I've been waiting this whole trip to say . . . Welcome . . . you have arrived!"

Signed,
Taybrianne

11
Identify Me As . . .

"He has identified us as his own by placing the Holy Spirit in our hearts as the first installment that guarantees everything he has promised us."

— 2 CORINTHIANS 1:22

YOUR NEW IDENTITY IS GOING TO BE IMPECCABLE! YOU HAVE to abandon any image of yourself that is not from God. No longer will people be able to identify you how they have in the past: whore, slut, ugly, fat, skinny, stupid, weak, dirty, unimportant . . . because this time they will have to change their approach toward you. People are not even going to be able to recognize you because of your new identity and your transformation into this beautiful woman. Your God-given identity is more important than what people called you out to be. Your God-given identity is more important because it holds more value than what this world tried to turn you into. Your God-given identity is important because it means that you are special, you were chosen, you are unique, and you are one of a kind.

Your true identity means to love yourself, flaws and all. It means to realize that you have been created with a purpose for a purpose. Don't be afraid to embrace your weaknesses. God's strength works best in our weaknesses . . . that's the *word*! So, it doesn't matter about you being weak; it gives God a reason to want to make you stronger. It means recognizing the potential that lies within. Your tone, your character, your smile, your personality are going to be vital in this next season to, as a whole, strengthen our young women, to inspire our rising queens to let them know how valuable and important they are. Don't look down upon yourself for not having it all together. That's the beauty of life! You will never have it all together, but every day, you learn more about who you are. If you begin to live right and become desperate to live a life that pleases God, your identity will become clear. God's words in James 4:8 say, "Draw close to me, and I'll come closer to you."

Each step that you take toward God, he's taking another step toward you. The bigger your steps, the bigger his steps! God knows your name! He knows who you are, so it does not matter about all the names they used to call you. There's a reason that word "used" is past tense, because it means that it's behind you. You are not defined by your feelings or emotions. You are not defined by your struggles or your circumstances. You are not defined by your successes or your failures. You are not defined by the environments that were abusive to you mentally and spiritually. *You can and you will come out!*

You must be careful because if you don't know who you are, you will become vulnerable to the opinions of others and what they consider you to be. Stand firm and know who you are! Stop accepting what "they" have said about you and start believing what God says about you. Believe him when he says that you were Fearfully and Wonderfully Made. Believe him when he says he created you in his image and in his likeness. Believe him when he says you are a royal priesthood; part of a *chosen* generation.

Your new identity conquers all those names that people ever called you. This new identity has the power to tear away all those labels that were ever attached to you! I promise you, knowing your identity in Christ is such beautiful feeling. You don't let negative words spoken over your life break you down anymore because you know who you are. Your appetite for spiritual growth begins to change. You live free by living your best life! Not only do you know who you are, but you know *whose* you are . . . and that is a child of God! Jesus was able to complete his ministry on Earth and fulfill his assignment because he knew who he was. He didn't allow negative words and evil plans of those who were so corrupt to break him or interrupt his assignment.

You don't let negative words spoken over your life break you down anymore because you know who you are. Your appetite for spiritual growth begins to change. You live free by living your best life!

God knows who you are. He knows you better than you know yourself. On a daily basis, pray and ask him to search your heart, mind, and spirit so that he can continue to reveal your identity to you. Don't bend or break the next time someone speaks negatively over your life or attempts to bring up your past. Respond out of love and not hate. Don't retaliate by trying to get even but pray for that individual! Your faith in God will continue to grow stronger the more you focus on your Identity in Christ! Your identity is valuable . . . *Protect it!* No matter what Satan tries to do to you to rupture who you are, know that you are stronger in Christ!

Always remember that no matter what life throws at you, your identity in *Christ* cannot be shaken, destroyed, or taken away from you. Ralph Waldo Emerson said, "The only person you are destined to become is the person you decided to be."

A Note from Tay:

"I am so proud of you! I know this journey has not been the best for you, but guess what? . . . You made it! And that's all that matters. It doesn't stop here. I told you in the letter that you must continue to let your light shine. So, keep shining, Beautiful!"

Signed,
Taybrianne

12

The Redefined Woman

*"I will praise thee; for I am fearfully
and wonderfully made: marvelous are thy works;
and that my soul knoweth right well."*

— Psalm 139:14 King James Version (KJV)

There is nothing more beautiful, nothing more amazing, nothing more impeccable, than a woman who can be unapologetic about being her true self. That is the essence of a woman with class, dignity, style, and grace. What is the definition of a redefined woman? A redefined woman is one who walks with confidence and walks in purpose. She is one who doesn't have to chase people or opportunities. Her light will cause people and opportunities to pursue her. She is the one who will most likely spend time walking alone, only to find herself in places that no one has ever been before.

Who Am I?

I'LL TELL YOU WHO I AM: MY NAME IS TAYLOR BRIANNE COHEN. After many years of being comfortable in that place of confinement, I found the strength and the courage to come out of hiding. Today, I no longer stand in front of the mirror in complete disgust with the way I look; instead I smile because this masterpiece that God has created is beautiful. This time when I stand in front of my mirror, I smile, and I speak life into that woman that I see. I command my spirit to *live* and everything that lies dormant to *get up!*

No longer am I the girl who is angry at herself because of her imperfections. I am not that girl anymore who has to wear clothes that are revealing or excessive amounts of makeup just for somebody to notice me. I embrace my thick and beautiful hair that continues to grow each day. I can't even tell you the last time that I had suicidal thought because of my insecurities and struggles with low self-esteem, because that girl is long gone. No more am I that girl who cries herself to sleep at night because she doesn't look the part. No longer am I the girl who tried to fit in, or only did this and that because everyone else was hip to it. No longer do I surround myself with negative influences that are not helping me to produce fruit that will remain. No longer do I seek the attention of others for people to hear me.

No more am I that girl who cries herself to sleep at night because she doesn't look the part. No longer am I the girl who tried to fit in, or only did this and that because everyone else was hip to it.

I *command* the attention in the room just by my presence alone, in the humblest way. I am bold, and I stand with Confidence. I *am* the *woman* who finally loves herself for who God created me to be. I am the woman who sees the potential that I have to turn this world upside down with what God has gifted me. I encourage myself even if nobody encourages me. (David encouraged himself and found strength in the Lord.) I don't have to dress a certain way or look the part just so people see me. No longer do I feel unimportant, unappreciated, or not good enough. *I am more than enough!*

I'm no longer intimidated by my future and my assignment. I know my purpose in life and why I was created. I know that God chose me specifically, and I accept being chosen. I love my family, and I am grateful that we were faced with some of the challenges years ago because it has made us all stronger. We have a better relationship because of it! I appreciate the pain that I experience from the attack from people with their negative words. When blessed with an opportunity to be in a room surrounded by many influential and successful people, *I own it!* This time when I ask myself that question, *Who am I?* I have an answer! My response is, I am a woman who has been Redefined, and not by this world but through Christ. I've been given another chance to get it right! I am an author who is going to not only write more books and travel across the world, but I am going to allow rising authors to be able to publish their books through my publishing company without having to fear that their work will immediately be rejected.

I am an entrepreneur who will have multiple businesses with a Christ-centered foundation that will not only impact and change lives forever, but I will have a legacy to be remembered by. I am the Woman who has been given new opportunities, more open doors, more seats at the table. I have made it a lifestyle to give back consistently, and I'm grateful for everything that life brings.

This time I stand by my truth! I stand up for this great and awesome woman I am. I respect who I am now more than ever. I understand that I am still on this road to greatness, and there are so many things that I still have not even seen yet. I am an inspirational influencer whom other young women will look up to for wisdom and insight on how to develop the strength and the courage to go from the girl to the *woman. I am* that woman who will teach this rising generation of young girls on how to develop a relationship with God, how to carry themselves as young women, how to *slay*, and, most importantly, how to remain a boss at all times! That's who I am!

Who Are You?

List five words that describe who you are and five words that describe what you are *not* . . .

I AM . . .

_____

_____

_____

_____

_____

I AM NOT . . .

_____

_____

_____

_____

_____

If I can impart any wisdom to you, it would be to always remain true to yourself. I cannot stress that enough. I see so many people, especially in this generation, completely losing it because they simply have no clue of who they are. They have looked to social media as validation of who they are based on how many likes they can get, leaving this perception to the outside world that "they got it," when in reality they are struggling to maintain the facade they have created. You do not have to be that kind of person. I know what it's like to get lost in the process, but don't stay lost. At some point you need to seek a new and healthier direction.

You do not have to live your life every day trying to be like someone else. Embrace who you are by living your own life. I thank God that I am not who I used to be—that girl who questioned herself all the time, *Who am I?* I am so thankful that I finally have an answer! I have an answer because the one who holds the answer showed me who I am. The only way for you to experience greatness is by being *you!* If nobody has ever told you, let me be the first person to tell you: You are beautiful, you are awesome, you are amazing, you rock, and your special gift is needed now more than ever. You got this.

I believe in the power of helping others and sharing what works for me. Although what works for me might not work for you, I still want to share with you some amazing suggestions for your life that you should try:

The first is journaling. I journal a lot. My mentor introduced it to me. Ever since, it has been a major "to do" in my life. Even with how busy my mentor is in being a wife, a mother, a first lady of the largest African-American church in Nashville, Tennessee, and operating her own business, at the end of the day she still finds time to journal. I can do it and you can do the same, too!

I suggest you buy a journal or notepad that nobody ever has to read. Keep it hidden in a special place. Write in it every morning—whatever comes to mind—when you wake up and every night before you go to bed. Jot down your thoughts, your emotions, how your day went, anything that made you mad . . . just write! It's one way that I communicate with God, and I absolutely love it. It is also self-therapeutic. Anytime I feel like I am under an enormous amount of pressure, I depend on my pen and my journal to be my stress eliminator.

There is not a quota of how many pages you have to write; you just write for however long you feel it is necessary. I also date and time each entry in my journal so that when I go back and read, it helps me to keep track of my personal growth.

Get a prayer partner or someone who can hold you accountable. Remember, *iron sharpens iron*. A prayer partner is someone you should look to who will hold you accountable with anything pertaining to your spiritual life. Since you are on this new route, you need someone who can help you balance your personal life with your spiritual walk. This should be someone who is willing to pray for you at any given moment, especially during those times when you need it the most. Don't let her/him just pray for you; you should pray for them as well. Pray for each other. We discussed the importance of prayer and how it still works, so invest in this relationship with someone you can trust.

Purchase a devotional book or a Bible (or both). This might be new for some of you, and I don't want to force it on you and say that you *need* a Bible, although at some point in your life you will want your own personal Bible. Meanwhile, a great place to start is with a devotional book, which can be very helpful. I have one by Joyce Meyer that I absolutely love. It is called *Hearing from God Each Morning: 365 Daily Devotionals—*

one devotion for each day of the year. What I like most about this devotional is that it has a scripture that begins each devotion, then she ends it with what you need to do for that day. It really helps me grow more in the Word, and I know that it will help you, too.

Spend some alone time with God. It can be in your car, your bedroom, your office, the shower, or even in the closet; wherever that place is for you, give God the time that he deserves. Create an area in your home, perhaps a small corner, where you can place inspiring sticky notes, your journal, Bible and/or devotional, and dedicate that area to God. Turn off everything and make it about him. Sometimes we don't even realize how much we are constantly moving without communicating with God . . . until something goes bad. Let's break the habit! For me, my special place is the shower. I feel that it's where I am most in tune with God. I can tell him what I want without having to worry about anybody listening to me. I pray to him, I cry to him, I sometimes scream, and I even sing me a good song while in the shower. That is my safe place. Think about where that place is for you.

Be wise about your circle of friends. We hear phrases such as "Bad company corrupts good character." Many times, that is absolutely true. Use wisdom when hanging around certain people. Other people's perceptions of you is almost always based on the company you keep—who your friends are. Don't allow friends that you hang around to destroy your character. You need people in your circle who are sharpening you, holding you accountable, who are there with you at your lowest, and who will be there when you reach your peak. But . . . it's imperative that you *are* careful of those rats! They only come around when they smell cheese.

It's Only *Up* from Here

You have been created to inspire others, no matter who you are or whatever mistakes you have made. There is someone out there in need of your inspiration. You can receive inspiration even while inspiring others. Let your story be a blessing to your own life. Let your wisdom and advice to others strengthen you, too. You do not have to sound a certain way or have a certain pedigree to be an inspiration. God can use anybody, so don't be afraid if he uses you! Let your light shine . . . *brightly*! There is no other way to go from here but *up*.

You got it! Every idea, dream, and vision will happen! If it doesn't happen right away, don't give up . . . don't you quit! You have come too far, and you have been through too much for you to just stop. Your brokenness was meant just for you! But there *is* a breakthrough around the corner with your name on it! Keep going, keep grinding, keep creating, keep dreaming, keep believing, keep *speaking*. It is going to happen at the right time, during the right season, for the right moment.

Someone is counting on you to *win*! And my sister, you *will* win! We will win together. Trust God and believe that he is ordering every step that you take. Jeremiah 29:11, one of my favorite scriptures, says, "For I know the plans that I have for you, declares the Lord, plans to prosper you and not to harm you, to give you a hope and a future." You have a great future ahead of you, and God's plan always win.

Back when I was in undergraduate school preparing for graduation and looking for a job, God spoke to me and said, "Unexpected blessings in unexpected places." Literally, that is how it has been for me. Ever since then, I am constantly reminding myself that my blessings from God are going to continue to be unexpected, coming from places where I least expected a blessing. I speak that over your life! Blessings are going to flow into your life from places you least expected. Stay in position and *be ready*! I am proud of you. I am proud of the woman that you are, and I am even more proud of the woman you will soon become.

That young girl who now looks up to you . . . yeah, she is counting on you, too! If you are a mother, your child is counting on you to make it. Continue down this route because this is a great road to be on. "Eyes have not seen and ears have not heard . . . " You will see so many amazing things on this route. *It's bigger, it's brighter,* and *it's better*! This is just the beginning . . .

Signed,
Taybrianne XOXO

A Prayer for You

F ATHER GOD, I THANK YOU FOR EVERY WOMAN WHO HAS READ this book from beginning to end. You are the Creator of Life! You are the Creator of Heaven and Earth. You have created us all in your image and in your likeness before we began forming in our mother's womb. It is my prayer that each woman that has read this book has been inspired in so many ways through this sharing of my testimony, my struggles, and the hidden secrets, words of encouragement, scriptures, and quotes to push them to their destination as Redefined Women. And *thank you* for giving me the courage to be able to be transparent in writing about those places of which I was previously afraid to speak. I pray that from this day on, no longer will these women look back or become a victim of the history from their past. *We are victors!*

I pray that they will snatch off every label and that *you* will break every chain that has ever kept them locked away physically, mentally, and emotionally. I speak that no longer will they live each day as "just the girl" but that they will embrace the newness that has just arrived. It is my prayer that they have received a better understanding of what it means to have an identity that is their own . . . that God-given identity. Remind them of who they are in *you*! I pray that this next season of their life will be the *best* season of their life.

I pray that they will love everything about who you have created them to be . . . flaws and all! Remind them that they are beautiful, intelligent, and simply amazing in their own unique and special way. I pray that they will learn how to forgive when it hurts so that they can walk into the season of freedom . . . *indeed*! Teach each woman to *demand* freedom over their life. To speak it out of their mouth and then to walk in it! Out of that hard place, let them continue to bless you and praise you! Let intentional prayer continue to sustain them. Help them to develop a hunger to live right!

It is my desire that every woman will begin to give birth to that special unique talent or gift that resides on the inside. Remove and block out any distraction before it even makes its way into their lives . . . We all have something to bring to the table, and it starts *now*! Let us walk into a room and *own* it! Let us grind! Let us come together as women and support one another.

Most importantly, Father, I pray that no matter where life takes them, or where you have them, that they will always stay true to themselves. Continue to cover them and keep them wherever you have them to be. Allow that greatness to continue to unravel every single day. Anoint every step that they take. Remind your daughters that they have been chosen by you with a purpose on purpose, and that one day the entire world will realize how special they are! We thank you for Grace . . . that very thing that none of us deserve. Without you, we are nothing! But with you, we have the power to become all that you want us to be.

In the name of Jesus Christ,
Amen!

Notes

1. Divecha, Diana PhD., "What Happens to Children When Parents Fight?", http://www.developmentalscience.com/blog/2014/04/30/what-happens-to-children-when-parents-fight. Sourced from E. Mark Cummings and Patrick Davies, *Marital Conflict and Children: An Emotional Security Perspective*, The Guilford Press, 2011.

2. The National Domestic Violence Hotline, "Get the Facts and Figures," http://www.thehotline.org/resources/statistics/, viewed May 9, 2018.

3. Love Is Respect, "Dating Abuse Statistics," http://www.loveisrespect.org/resources/dating-violence-statistics/, viewed May 9, 2018.

4. O'Connor, Carol, *Secrets of Great Leaders: The 50 Strategies You Need to Inspire and Motivate*, Teach Yourself, 2016.

About the Author

A UTHOR TAYLOR BRIANNE COHEN, A NATIVE OF RACINE, WISCONSIN, earned a bachelor of science degree in public health from Tennessee State University and is studying for her master's degree in organizational leadership at Lipscomb University in Nashville, Tennessee.

‌⤳

www.ingramcontent.com/pod-product-compliance
Lightning Source LLC
Chambersburg PA
CBHW030934090426
42737CB00007B/421